Poetic Art

Paul Claudel

POETIC ART

Sicut creator, ita moderator.
Donec universi seculi pulcritudo . . .
velut magnum carmen ineffabilis
modulatoris.

S. AUGUSTIN, EP. V,
ad Marcellinum.

Translated by Renee Spodheim

PHILOSOPHICAL LIBRARY
NEW YORK

PRINTED IN THE UNITED STATES OF AMERICA

CONTENTS

Knowledge of Time

KNOWLEDGE OF TIME

ARGUMENT

PRELUDE.—Interpretation of the universe and of the shape that simultaneous things weave around us.

I. ON CAUSE.—Definition by means of the idea of continuity. Analysis of the notion of cause. The couple: *subject—means*. Examples and classification. Comparison with the couple, major and minor premise, of the syllogism. The subject does neither imply, nor control the means. Forms, not laws. Eternal newness of things. Their recurrence indicates the supreme and sacred importance the Creator conferred upon them, as upon words of the eternal vocabulary. All each thing needs, is to exist. Discussion of the Mechanism, absurdity of perpetual movement as an end in itself. Resumé: The subject does not carry a plan of action within itself and finds one only through deciding upon a certain effect, offered by the means. Generating difference.

II. ON TIME.—Space or the completed design, time or the design which is about to take shape in a universal motion, that is time. The Universe is a time-recording machine. Comparison with human clocks: movement, regulator, recording devices, etc. The primal motion is always *from* rather than *toward*. Double time of each movement, impulse from the outside, tendency towards repetition. Solar escapement. The origin of motion is to be found in the quivering of matter in contact with a different reality, which is the Spirit: the fear

3

of God. All motion is time and serves to mark it. Time considered as a continuous movement or duration. Modes and phases of time. Continuation and advance in duration. The past is the forever-growing total of conditions of the future, which is, thus, always new and as yet unknown.

III. ON THE HOUR.—The hour within me, the hour for which I stand and which I am, not only in time but in duration. This very movement, in a heart whose horizons, in perspective around it, are but the reflections and concentric interpreters. My intention in the plan as a whole. How much do I know about it? What do I know of my affinity with things and of that of things among themselves, considered solely from the point of view of simultaneity? The Harmonic Cause or movement, which regulates the assembly of beings at a given moment of duration. It is the Nature of Poetry. The new Logic, expressing itself by metaphors. In addition to their own realities, and to the relationship they maintain with others, all things stand as symbols and expressions of the moment reached in duration.

CONCLUSION.—Time is the invitation to die, the means by which all things are able, on the threshold of eternity, to confess their naught in their Creator's bosom.

I am not considering the future, for it is the present the gods urge us to penetrate. Now and then, a man raises his brow, sniffs, listens, considers, finds his position: he thinks, sighs, and, taking his watch out of his vest pocket, reads the time. *Where am I? What time is it?* these are the inexhaustible questions we ceaselessly ask the world. *Where am I? What have I achieved?* In order to answer these questions, each ancient city had its own augur. Under way, against the tide, the human vessel was on the watch. Nothing in vain. Man thought that all things—at all times and with his secret consent, incited by the same impulse which measures his own growth—worked out a mystery which had to be intercepted, of necessity. And this is why the diviner armed his hand and went to look for it even in the bowels of animals, so that a being endowed with an intelligible voice might captivate the exhalation of earth and the belch of the abyss! The sibyl knew how to deceive with her handful of dead leaves, sowing the seed of words into the wind. Each religious site concealing an oracle—as others conceal their springs of healing—had a temple to exploit it. And, in our days, the same curiosity invents instruments, and builds hypotheses and observatories. Everywhere, and at every moment, each of us knows what degree the temperature reaches and the weight of the air which presses us down. The whole skin of the earth has become as sensitive as the tips of our fingers and wires news of stormy weather and serene skies. The Bulletin dealing with spots on the sun plays an important part in the stock-market and in politics. The Globe still sets the hand removed from its own mass. And thus, we are always perfectly informed on the weather, such as it is at the present moment and on its future behavior, on the agreements concluded between Phoebus and the clouds for the entire day. But when the occultation of our own daily sun enables us to find our position in the absolute, how naive the practice of astrology, compared with our tables and our methods and these strong eyes we point to the celestial landmarks. What almanac has ever favorably compared with the one of the Bureau of Longitudes and what horoscopic theme bearing the motto of Saturn or the Crab, with the more closely knitted figures drawn in regular columns? We read better the meaning of radiant skies. An immense, a total hour, calculated every moment, is more decisive than the one which, in days of old, established the birth of kings, delayed battles, presided at the gathering of medicinal plants, favored purgings.

We do not hang our politics and our cooking on stars anymore. Nevertheless, everything that happens has a special place in duration, according to a given combination of irreproducible sidereal numbers, just as each point is determined on the map by its distance from the meridian line and from the equator, and finds its arithmetic root in the infinite skies. But it may well be that, closer than stars and planets, all shifting and animated things surrounding us, are to be trusted as much and bear in them the scattered evidence of the inner impulse which makes our own life that which it is.

And this is the mystery which is now to be put on paper with the blackest of inks.

ON CAUSE

Whenever something appears before our eyes or in our intelligence, our spirit itches to classify it, on the spot, in the drawer in which it belongs, to insert it into the continuum. *Cause* is the articulation we strive to discover; it is all this with a productive energy without which no given thing could be.

These words circumscribe the sense and the area of our investigation. We shall not try to understand the mechanism of things from underneath, like a stoker crawling on his back under his locomotive. But we shall look upon the creatures as a whole, as a critic upon the work of a poet, enjoying it fully, examining the means by which his *effects* are obtained, like an artist, admiring, with eyes half-shut, the work of another artist, like an engineer looking upon the work of a beaver. The four causes of the Philosopher, the material, the formal, the final, the efficient, do not have any place here. To look for the cause of each entity upheld by a name is simply to envisage the *matter* and the *means*.

A deafening adage, reducible to mere noise, fills the pages of all books: *No effect without cause!* But would you dare, oh, empty cricket, warble as loudly between my fingers: *No cause without effect?* I do not expect you to do so, I merely smile, while repeating after you: Yes, no effect without *causes*. Without *causes*, in the plural.

For there is never one single cause. The series of abstractions brings us back to the pristine ideas of movement and mass, of engine and motion, or, more roughly, of an external influence, manifested on all given things, by a local movement. This coupling of a subject and of an action exerted from the outside on the subject constitutes the real cause. Arrangement with infinite possibilities of variation in its modes, according to each effect to be achieved.

Let us make a more minute examination.

The characteristic of the subject is that its value, its "power," is more general in scope than the effect achieved by applying the means.—At the mouth of the Phaeacian harbor, the sea, wielded by the wind, has indulged in giving the shape of a boat to the bone projecting out of the ancient body of the Earth.—Hydrogen has its own properties, and so has oxygen. The ratio one to two is needed so that the combination may take place and form water.—A living spark, the microbe, is needed, to produce, out of oxygen united with nitrogen, nitrate, the food of grass.—The earth needs the seed to convert its inert flesh into a soluble sugar.—The mother's blood needs the germ for the conception of the animated clot.—Marble and steel need the sculptor, the artisan with his tools to carve out the statue and to assemble the engine.

As is shown by an analysis of these proofs, by the mere fact of being created, all creatures, in turn, are creators, depository, under the new commandment they embrace, of a figurative power ready to spring forth. The intervention of the means, that is, of the external or latent work of its precise fiat, like an articulate order, unriddles the subject, constrains and determines it.

The means may be classified according to their mode of operation: I append the following outline:

1. *So-called fortuitous cases and application of means to an end they do not imply.*

   A powder magazine—lighting—explosion.
   The bulk of the earth—wind, rain, frost—erosion phenomena, carving of the surface of the earth.
   Napoleon and his army—Russian winter—doom of the Emperor, his down-fall.
   Natural chemical reactions.

2. *Unconscious application of means to an end.*

   a—*Earth—seed—plant.*
   Food—the digestive system—chyle, blood.
   Honey and its container—egg—larva.
   The phenomena of crystallization and those of primitive instincts.

   b.—*Ovaries at work—the industry of laying eggs and making nests—insect, bird, fish, the food they provide for the carnivorous species.*

3. *Conscious and voluntary application of means to an end.*

    a.—Application of instruments or processes to matter.
        Prey—hunting, teeth—meal.
        Marble—chisel—statue.
        Methods for the training of athletes.

    b.—To set forth voluntarily and start a natural series.
        Agriculture, medicine, breeding, physiological
          experiments, etc.

    c.—Creation of an artificial series.
        Clock, machine.

The first category defines the fortuitous or repeated meeting of subject and means, rather than an application; the next two consist of a real application of one to the other in view of a well determined purpose. The first four examples of the second category describe, between the two terms, an assimilation of substance to substance; in the last one there is no modification anymore, no sowing of means, but rather adaptation to the subject of an effort independent of the practitioner, toward an independent end, more or less completely ignored by him. Finally, in the third category, there is, with the knowledge of the term, choice, direction, arrangement of means. The means does not act alone, by virtue of the force vested in it; it is handled from the outside, it becomes a mere instrument. It does not in-

vent its effect by itself. From this point of view, it re-
veals an analogy with the first category.

The preceding clearly leads to this first conclusion:
The subject does not imply the means. How then are
they related to one another?

The three terms to which we have reduced the causal
action suggest at once to the mind the classical formula
of human reasoning, the syllogism. The syllogism is the
operation by means of which we recognize things and
recognize ourselves among them. In order to achieve
this, we give them a name, that is, we lay down the
specific qualities which distinguish them from all others.
We do not admit any others to the name we have coined
unless they conform to the conditions we have set down.
Instructed by experience, enlightened by certitude or
stimulated by our fantasy, we promulgate our will, we
decree, in the major premise, that a given quality is to
be attributed to the predicate of our choice; in the minor
premise, we certify that a given being or fact of reality,
fully corresponds to the description of our predicate; in
conclusion, we award to it, explicitly, the quality which
rightly belongs to it. The members of the syllogism are
thus perfectly linked together, of necessity. The proposal we formulated has thus, indeed, the authority of
a *law*. We are not masters of the phenomena, but we
have the power and the right to give them names, and
to stipulate the conditions under which these names
will be applied to them. It rigorously follows that if a

phenomenon complies with all the conditions represented under a name, it possesses, among others, the particular condition we detach for a moment in order to give it special attention. This does not, in any way, mean that the method through which we find our way in the dictionary of nature is the same through which nature itself found the terms and agglomerated the meanings.

But logical investigation makes one point clear: namely, that a thing can be *defined* only and that it exists *only through the traits* which make it different from all others.

Like the syllogism, the causal formula proceeds from the general to the special. A scattered, inoperative major premise is joined by the means which determine it, just as the minor premise describes the passage from the potential to act. But they are not attached by any logical necessity; in other words, it is not impossible to think of one without thinking of the other. On the contrary, their operation is conditioned by this very difference. No thing is complete in itself and each can only be completed by that which it lacks. But that which each particular thing lacks is infinite; we cannot know, in advance, the complement it calls for. Only through the secret taste of our spirit, do we realize when effective harmony is achieved, that is, the essential and generating fundamental difference.

Our mind conceives and names the general only.

When we describe to someone a person we met, so as to make him realize who it was, we use a multitude of features; each of them is general, but, as a whole, they all can refer only to the specific person: a small man, brown hair, beard of such and such a color and form, wearing clothes of such and such a type. But all the features used for a better identification of anything, animate or inanimate, its habits or its qualities, its relationship to the outside world, are not less organic, nor is their value less permanent than its intrinsic structure. The fact alone is offered to our eyes as it is to our mind. It fills the entire space and emerges, by exclusion, as the all-important trait. We see the causes and effects as a whole in one single block before us, like a naked man and his limbs, and we conclude that the same *law* regulates the existence of things and controls their coming into being, that an irrepressibly determined generating power is instilled into the things themselves. An error which is contradicted by the absolute condition of the essential and complementary difference, and the principle we upheld here: *form*, not *law*.

(*Form;* in the sense in which it is used in expressions like: the form of the hand, the form of this vase).

Beings and things, and the different combinations, which, under the name of phenomena, facts, events, settle in an interlacing relationship in time and form together a sort of cloth that a hand would eternally pull out of its roll. This cloth is the object of our eyes, of our attention; of our mind; it is the object of our science. We realize that its pattern runs smoothly and without flaws, and we hasten to formulate the principle: *nihil ex nihilo;*—meaning that there is a natural and constant relationship between certain *motives*, as between a flower and its stem, between a hand and its arm; *nihil sine causa sufficienti;*—in a word, we hold the means of evaluating phenomena, of submitting them, in their advance, to a steady term of comparison, of classifying them according to universal numbers: *nihil absque pondere et mensura.* By reason of their very definition, by their very structure, these weights and these measures, these frames, these tables, these meridians and these artificial horizons have a general and absolute rigidity, a mathematical stability. But all this equipment and the laws we infer from them are merely instruments of criticism, schemes of simplification, means of intellectual assimilation. They possess no generating power and no compulsory value in themselves.

Teacher! The light in your classroom is excellent and the lamp-shades filter just the right amount on the copybooks the students fatten with your doctrine. But, do not forget! man is still naked. Under his lewd garments, he is as pure as a stone! I can be satisfied neither with the shining color of your blackboard, nor with the faint marks of chalk. What I need is the black sky itself! Ah, to be able to smash the window with the weight of my entire body! What I need are the nations of the Space, the display of "terms" as yet incalculable! Everything is known, you say, everything can be learned. The work will soon be completed and published; we advise our subscribers that the last volumes of our Encyclopedia are about to appear. Everything can be easily explained, and the phenomena of nature are but a demonstration —similar to that made on a blackboard—of the laws I have had the privilege to expound before you. Oh, foolish mind who thinks that nothing can ever be exhausted as an object of knowledge! Let me tell you: you did not drain the genius of its liberty and joy! The sea keeps its treasures to itself; Apollo still haunts the forge of Thunder! Open your eyes! The world is still unscathed, unblemished as it was when it came into being, as fresh as milk! The unknown is the subject matter of our knowledge, it is the blessing of our mind and its cherished food. The men who lived before us did not harm our right, they left our patrimony untouched. Things are not like the parts of a machine, but rather like the forever active elements of an always new drawing. Man does not come to know the world by that which he extorts from it, but rather by that which he adds to it: himself. Man creates the harmony which is the very substance of his knowledge, like a key-board on which I let my fingers wander.

We have defined the idea of necessity; we have reduced it to the series of solidary conditions each thing must fulfill in order to be endowed with a name. In reality, this name represents merely the confidence we put in nature, our certitude of always finding it identical to itself, at least as substance of our knowledge. We are sure of our vocabulary; neither the nouns, nor the intransitive or active verbs which express their actions and relationships will fail to carry out their mission. Hours and seasons always carry the same stock of adjectives and adverbs. Thus it follows, from the persistence with which nature upholds or repeats the vocables concealed in her pages that they have a particular value, an indispensable meaning, a typical, sacramental importance and authenticity, and, that they are the predetermined object of the activity they name. The effect alone is truly a peremptory and pure necessity included in this aim—that is the effect—and the series of causes is but an aspect of the operation carried out for its achievement. The thing bursts forth, a new and self-explanatory creation, and the permanent command: Let this be! still stirs the innermost feelings of creation. (A commandment our science mimics; and our experiments are but clumsy questions.) While you watch the movement of a machine, I enjoy playing an instrument. There are no laws, there are only recipes.

Let us take apart this "machine" by means of which school masters want to pre-figure our "task," making it thus into an obsession of servile minds, by way of which the universe works and, undoubtedly, deserves to be.

Every machine, alive or manufactured, finds its nourishment and its purpose outside itself (I except the clock
whose beats guide this poem), the latter differing from
the first insofar as it is being strictly determined *ad
unum*. This double servitude of the power to be captured and of the product to be yielded conditions the
minute fitting of its parts and the uniform sequence
of its performances, the machine itself. But the Universe as a whole and according to your postulate does
not include any external element. What then is this
power without a source, this self-feeding and self-
created machine? A toy, marching on, with no other
purpose than its very movement, driven solely by its in-
ability to stop. Behold the eternal automaton, in its
eternal dance!—The machine is but a grouping of means,
between the two ends it implies.

To conclude: each cause is a combination, not necessarily implied in any of the component terms. It does
not engender its generating effect. The world is not the
unquenchable development of a principle, the expansion of the atom, the spontaneous combustion of an
equation. There is nothing within bodies, compelling
them, at a crucial moment of their existence, to generate
continuance. The formulae I copy in my book can no
more bring forth the fact than can the shadow of a
mirror be limited by saying the Lord's Prayer back-
wards or the names of the devils *Setos* and *Crepo*. Our
discerning a few conditions of a fact does not mean that

we are in possession of the reasons for its existence.
We see it better or worse: that is all. Oxygen com-
bines with another gas, just as the arm is joined to the
hand. Kepler's laws are but an abstract representation,
a mathematical drawing of the movement of a body in
space, an abbreviated formula, a mnemotechnical con-
vention. The buoyant force on a body when partly or
wholly submerged is equal to the weight of the liquid
it displaces: this is a law, on the same grounds as the
following assertion: if I push my fingers down my
throat I will be sick. The only difference between
these two unvarying phenomena is that the first one is
simpler, and can therefore be expressed in numbers. A
law can be established whenever we perceive a reliable
and unvarying proportion.

A proportion, that is, a difference: a cause is fundamentally that. It is the achievement or the breaking of
the equilibrium between two terms, the satisfaction of
a need, the composition of an accord. It is not positive,
it is not included in the subject. It is what the subject
lacks most. And what does the individual lack more
than being complete?

My wealth is inexhaustible! For wanting the whole
universe and its wanting me means owning the whole
universe.

II

ON TIME

THIS IS HOW things manage to exist; nothing changes, nothing begets by itself, but by means of receiving the complement it needs as an unadulterated gift. But no matter what the work already accomplished, the thing exists, here it is: everything resulted in a name; it all came to this, to a form, the production of a certain kind of tangible figure and form. Let us accept it as it is. All figures are limited *ex intra* by the amount of matter they contain, and outwardly by the other terminal forms which surround them; they belong to a solid, coherent, indivisible whole, in which they settle and fit. Since the essence of *causes* is studied, why close my eyes to the consideration of things on a horizontal plane, to the appreciation of the *motifs* which adorn and make up the moment? It is the picture which gives its value to the spot. But the drawing is not completed. We see it in the making before our own eyes. It is not enough to understand the whole, the completed figure in its features, we must consider the developments it implies, as the bud implies the rose, catch the intention and the purpose, the *direction and the sense*. Time is the *sense* * of life.

---

* TRANSLATOR'S NOTE: In French, the double connotation of sense, namely *meaning* and *direction* are equally strong. Since the author plays on words repeatedly, the translator has often found it necessary to leave "sense" for both meanings.

(*Direction and sense* as in the direction of a stream, the sense of a sentence, the sense of smell).

The hand of a writer covers the paper from beginning to end in a uniform motion. A million different words, lending strength and color to each other, owe their life to this uniform motion, so that the entire mass, in its fluid steadiness, feels each contribution of the moving pen. In the same way, a pure movement exists in the skies, whose earthly reflection is expressed by a transcription of infinite variety. A body cannot be at once in two different places; it must therefore visit them in succession. In other words, it must cease *to be* there if it is *to be* here. Why this change of place and what is the meaning of the words *here* and *there?* Elsewhere, the presence of another body which controls it. A single position does not exhaust the relations uniting them. The mere fact that two different bodies exist in space produces movement, which can be defined as the independent study each of them makes in comparing itself to the other one. What is the link between these bodies? this movement? who beats the time? where is the spring and the regulator?

I declare that the whole universe is nothing but a time-marking machine. Let us consider, in this light, the human instruments, which are but unwitting copies of the total clock, and the inserting in a box, by means of nails and cog-wheels, of the same power which drives the great chariot of the Moon and of the other Gods.

Three elements are combined in it: the movement, its regulator making for uniform escapement up to the last fraction of its duration, the recording device, or the wheel, which expresses it by its revolution. There are two types of movement: the descent or recoil of a weight or of a spring: it uses the sense of a direction through a body, or the reaction of a bent blade, and, offering always the same obstacle to overcome, it counts its successive strokes. What is the use of the wheel, which, from its stationary center, transmits to each point of its disc, the impulse it receives in but one point, modifying the position, without altering the distance? But what is the nature of the movement, and its origin at bottom?

Motion can be considered at its beginning or at its end, depending on whether it goes or comes. But considered purely in itself, it is primarily a change of place, the departure of a body from the point it had occupied at first. There can be no reasons inherent in the very nature of the body for its moving from the spot in which it had first settled. Its choosing of a new place must therefore be due to a stronger, external power; it yields to coercion. But from the trajectory its follows there results a sense of natural direction, or gravity, and the tendency of retracing its steps. And such is the origin of motion, in the skies and in clocks, such is the initial pulsation.

That is why the sun, stopping on its own axis, caught fire, in the center of the world; ecstasy in violence!

like a lamp which is lit, like someone looking all around, in an effort to find out where he is. But absolute displacement, unfolding painfully, its core struggling in the compensation of a double effort, is translated by a displacement of the various parts of the peripheric mass in relation to itself, and the direct axial movement withdrawing, drawing nearer, the vibratory throbbing, is expressed by a fly-wheel; rotation for a single body; translation on a pivot, for a compound system. How can we admit, for a moment, overcoming the reluctance of our mind to assimilate anything different from that which the eye sees, certain myths, such as that created by Empedocles, for instance, or by Laplace? and, in spite of the principle that nothing can be born out of nothing or is differentiated by itself, shall we admit the nebula, and that potter's wheel on which planets are supposed to have molded themslves? Could we dream that seeds of worlds, buried in chaos, might have acquired a shape and have developed, like a crystal that creates and a plant that grows? Or, when not even a watch can keep good time if the least important part of its wheel-work stops functioning, are we to believe that the machine, dedicated—not to the marking, but to the making of time could start oscillating without its weights and fly-wheels being adjusted and regulated? I defined weight as the *sense of sense*; for planets, it is the acknowledgment of their vital center. Following the impulse which drives it through space, the sun must surmount, with its own weight, the opposition of the planets, which hug and "wind him up," allied with him in his resistance. And their journey together is both the inscription of time in space, an expression of solar passion, and the escapement of the primordial distension.

Let us keep our mind on these last words.

The movement of a body means its leaving the place it had first occupied. It is therefore, as we have already stated, in itself, and first of all, an escape, a retreat, a withdrawal before a superior external force. It is the effect of intolerance, the impossibility of remaining on the same spot, of staying put, of subsisting. And so is dissipated, in inarticulate words, which do not touch our lips, the thought that, just as the conscious perception,[1] according to which I am the combination of a body and a soul, the origin of movement is in the shivering which takes hold of matter in contact with this different reality: the Spirit. It is the expansion of a handful of stars in space; and the source of time, the fear of God, the essential repulsion, recorded by the engine of the worlds.[2]

But if movement and time be homologous expressions of one and the same fact, any animated motive power of one of them would point toward the other and be part of the whole chronometric machinery. It also fol-

[1] Knowledge of the East. *On the Brain.*
[2] Initium sapatientiae timor Domini-Primus in orbe Deum novit timor.

lows that time has an objective reality, an origin and a
development, as shown by the progress of the hands on
a dial, a concrete and unique existence. Accordingly,
we can consider it either in its absolute duration and
its uniform flow, or in its material texture, in its continuity and its rhythm. That much, first. Let us begin
by considering how it is made. Let us examine the
elements of our human time.

During the revolution it accomplishes on its poles, the
Globe presents in succession all the points of its surface
to the sun. This exposure is our day. The progress and
the decline of light during the time we need to emerge
from night, on our way back to it, is translated by everything that absorbs it, as clearly, as minutely as by the
shadow of the gnomon or by the carrying over of the
angle on the circle. The color of the sky and of the land,
the feel of the earth under my feet, the flower which
opens and closes, the attitude and shade of the vegetation, the activity of animals and men, all these, together
with a certain common air, fill the tiniest divisions of this
pure time which ticks in our waistcoat pocket. The day
is the earth wallowing in the sun; the year is one of its
pirouettes, the salute to its King, the roundelay which
draws it closer or farther from his perpetual face; the
seasons, its attitudes. The position of the planet in its
orbit, its inclination on the ecliptic are shown as dis-
tinctly by this fruit I pick, by this fire about to be lit,
as by astronomical calculation. The rhythm of the winds,

the migration of mackerels and of swans, the greenery or the snow, the awakening of the vegetative power, the knowledge of the little shrub, waiting for its humble moment to bloom, the rut of quadrupeds and the song of all birds, the scorching heat of summer, the rich cadence of autumn, all these remain within the boundaries of measure, keep *time*, take up and impel the sentence begun elsewhere, set forth and sustain the theme, come to the final conclusion; all these correspond to a given aspect of the mathematical sky, to a given intersection of the horizon with night. And each day of each month, the satellite which officiates during our pilgrimage, comes to report on our position; the moon, like a scout we have taken with us, and like a fire whose brightness and eclipse continuously checked by the navigator, tells us how much time was needed to bring forth entirely our part of earth or to conceal it from the eyes of the sun, which is.

At each hour of the Earth, however, all hours exist at once; no matter what the season, all seasons live at once. While the seamstress sees noon on the dial of the Tower of Saint Eustache, the first low rays of the sun pierce the Virginian leaf; squadrons of cachalots frolic under the southern moon. It rains in London, it snows over Pomerania, while Paraguay is all roses, while Melbourne roasts. It seems that whatever exists can never cease existing, and that even time, meant to express existence under its fleeting aspect, implies a permanent,

irresistible necessity, each of its component parts having, as already stated, a concrete form and an individual
womanlike countenance.

Thus, such are the ways and bearing of time, which
brings and creates all things. But, while the hour com-
pressed in a case, leaves no trace of its passage other than
a certain fatigue of the springs, a certain wear of the
sprocket-wheels, the total, the creative hour, achieves
serious work, obtains results, makes a history we can
read. The sediment deposited on the bottom of the sea,
the toil of coral and termites, the migration of peoples
and the fall of empires, all happening at once on the
globe, white and black in turn, keeping pace with the
year, in their place on the sidereal space, are parts of
the same scheme, develop the same revelation. Through
the medium of equal days, in the forever resumed
rhythm of years, something that has started already endures and follows its course. The preparing of the soil to
be worked by means of fire and water, the reactions of
acids and salts, the spiral pull of vegetation, the animal
subdued by its instinct, man standing upright: all con-
verge toward the same design, receive from the same
motor, impulse, moderation and life. The freedom of
rational men is no less necessary to the common work
than the passivity of matter and the submission of
beasts. I compare it to the "recoveries" of the body which
maintains its equilibrium on the unstable soil, to the
writing hand which converts into words the movement

animating it. The task of the world is to go on, to manage its own continuity. To be is to create. All things
living in time listen, concert and compose. The meeting
of physical forces and the play of human will cooperate
in the construction of the mosaic of Instant.

And thus, Time is not merely the perpetual renewal
of days, of months and years; it is the artisan of something real, which grows with every second, the *Past*,
that which has once been given life. All things have to
exist, in order to cease existing, in order to make room
for the subsequent which they call forth. The past is an
incantation of things to come, the generating difference
they need, the forever growing sum of future conditions. It determines the *sense*, and, in this light, it does
not cease existing anymore than the first words of a
sentence when the eye reaches the last ones. Better still,
it does not stop developing, organizing within itself, like
a building, whose role and aspect is changed by new
constructions, or like a sentence made clearer by another
sentence. In a word, what has been once, never loses its
operating virtue; it increases with each moment's contribution. The present minute is different from all other
minutes, in that it does not border on the same quantity
of past. It does not explain the same past, it does not
imply the same future. I continue more than the ances-
tor whose follower I am. At every breath, the world
remains as new as it was at the first gulp of air out of
which the first man made his first expiration.

III

ON THE HOUR

It strikes and I reverberate. At this explosion of the clock, I and all things that exist have the same quantity of past behind us; a certain mass removed from the possible is gone, never to be changed again, a claim on the future. It is a beat that awakens me; I become conscious of that which surrounds me; the tide of the universe reached a certain line marked in advance. I am. I am, but what? I am, but where? What time is it within and outside me, according to my closing or opening myself?

I hear my heart within me, and the clock in the very middle of the house.

I am. I feel, I listen, within myself, to the beating of this machine, confined between my bones, a machine through which I continue to be. I "walk," by means of a movement, over which I have no control; who wound my inner spring? who set my heart? for how many hours is it supposed to serve me? which one have I reached? Whether I be asleep or awake, it does not cease to work for me, to take care of everything. The pump gathers my blood, at each suction, and compresses it, set afire by the respiratory sun to the four ends of my body. And I shall not be able to restrain for long the soaring of my ribs. Suddenly, I choke, the base of the diaphragm extends, I draw air through the nostrils, and after having

combined with me, it is expelled as my breath, resound-
ing or noiseless, whether I speak or not, psychic spirit
and mist on a mirror. And as flame blazes under the
bellows, so do, with each inspiration, the life of the body
and that of the soul, the substantial verse, sentence or
action. Such is the rhythm within us, which burns us, so
that we may live, the anchor of our escape. And just
as the spring of the chronograph, regulated according
to the sun, presses, as it expands, against the system
of wheels and cogs, which touch the hands on the dial,
so the throbs of our heart bring about the hour we mark,
the hour we are.

And the hour, indicated on the enamel or the cal-
endar, marks the common position of things in duration,
of days, of years. June, Noon. After completing the
round, the indifferent hands start on another run. Tomorrow, on the circle of figures, the same line will an-
nounce Midnight. And on the very dial of Earth, from
year to year, July is determined by similar features.
Never, however, is it the same July, the same Midnight.
Under the closed rhythm of day and season, there exists
an absolute hour, carried over on a straight line, the
symbol of which is a forever growing number. Under
that which starts all over again, is that which goes on.
Our life, from birth to death, is but a division of this
absolute duration. It carries within itself, it has been
entrusted once and for all, with the principle of its beginning and of its end. The matter, in its rough form,

persists, the plant and even the animal are part of the
cycle of the year, the history of which they make, like
the jack, coming out of the watch-tower to strike the
quarter- and the half-hours on the clock; man alone
marks no other hour but his own. He feels, he has,
within himself, the very movement, circumferentially
reported by its successive horizons, widening around
it.[1] The appearance of the skies and of earth, the sun
going to sleep in the foliage, and the leaves themselves,
the moon shining bright on tall chrysanthemums are
just as much the consequence and the effect of the beating of man's heart as his very face, youthful or bearded.
A new astrological system! stars are not deciding on our
destiny any more, according to the horoscopic decree;
on the contrary, the stars, themselves, obey the heredi-
tary palpitation delegated to this receptacle of life under
my ribs. Something within me counts, adds one, completes the critical number for which the horses of the
sun are waiting, in order to hasten to their harness. I
know that I was created to measure a certain portion of
duration. Below the things that come to pass, I am conscious of this part of the total intention entrusted to me.
I am made for a purpose, each minute of my life is calculated for a contact, according to the play of my freedom, like each spiral of a spring wound around a barrel.
In paying attention to my intention, I find knowledge.
I appear and I cease to be on the spot and at the moment

[1] Spiritus vadens et non rediens—Ps. 77, 45.

when necessary for the pattern and the purpose which
need me.

A long time ago, in Japan, while going up from
Nikko to Chuzenji, I saw, juxtaposed by my line of
vision, although at great distance from each other, the
green of a maple tree filling the separating space, in
order to answer the appeal of a pine, asking for an agreement. These pages are meant to be the beginning of
a text on forests, the arborescent enunciation by June,
of a new Art of Poetry [1] of the Universe, of a new Logic.
The old one used syllogisms as an instrument of expression, the new one uses metaphor, the new word,
the operation resulting of the sole, conjoint and simultaneous existence of two different things. The
first one has a general and absolute affirmation as
a starting point, the attribution, once and for all, of a
quality, of a property to the subject. No matter what the
time and place, *the sun shines, the sum of the angles
of a triangle is equal to two right angles*. It creates abstract individuals, by defining them; it establishes invariable series between them. Its method consists in
naming. All these terms, once chosen, classified
according to type and species in the columns of
its repertory, after individual analysis, are applied
to all subjects brought to its attention. I compare this kind of logic to the first part of grammar, which

[1] Poiein, to make.

determines the nature and function of the different words. The second Logic would be more like the syntax of such a grammar, teaching the art of fitting words together and is practiced before our eyes by nature itself. There is only one science, that of the general, there is no creation, but of the particular. The metaphor,[2] the fundamental iambus or the connection between a flat and a sharp does not play only in the pages of our books: it is the autochthonous art used by all that which is born. And do not call it chance. The plantation of this bouquet of pines, the shape of this mountain are no more due to chance than the Parthenon or this diamond, in the cutting of which the lapidary grows old, but the product of a treasure of richer and more scholarly aims. I quote various proofs of geology and climate, natural and human history; our achievements and the means we use do not differ from those of nature. I understand that no thing survives by itself, but in its infinite relationship with all others. When I shall have taken apart all the organs of a plant or an insect, I shall still not know everything, any more than I shall know everything about the Misanthrope or the Miser from their silhouettes on the scenery. I shall still have to find out in what respect *this particular* leaf, *this particular* insect is essentially different from others, and thus why it is necessary, *what it is doing here*, its position in the whole, its part in the

[2] With its transpositions in the other arts: "values," "harmonies," "proportions."

plot of the play. The cherry-tree and the herring are not so prolific merely for themselves, but for the plundering hordes they feed. Time *goes by*, people say, yes: *something goes on*,[3] an infinitely complex drama, with intermingled actors, introduced or impelled by the action itself. Let a critic stop in front of the gaping stage! he will not see a series of isolated automatons indefinitely repeating the same gesture, but a common action, a continuous production of *commedia dell' arte*. My own entrance and exit are well marked; my cues are all settled. There, every thing, every being is represented by its own name, its specific weight in the surroundings in which it is cast, its total value as a symbol of the moment when the action takes place. You tell me about Waterloo, you explain the map to me, you narrate to me the meeting between Wellington and Blücher: and there is, indeed, a tie among these notions. And, I see Waterloo; and, over there, in the Indian Ocean, I see, at the same time, a pearl-diver, with his head suddenly cutting the water, close to his catamaran. And there is a relationship between these two happenings also. Both write down the same hour, both are ornaments belonging to the same design.

Let us follow the example of the nun Chaldea, and turn our eyes towards the absolute sky, on which the stars have drawn our birth certificate, in inextricable

[3] TRANSLATOR'S NOTE: As already stated, the author's predilection for playing on words makes it often necessary to use certain expressions, although others would seem more suitable.

figures and keep a record of our covenants and our oaths. But since we lack the polar star to give us the position, planets to indicate the bearing, sextants and horizons, look: your destiny lies in the heart of these unknown people who describe their trajectory, next to you, as much as it lies in the stars. The horseshoe you pick up out of the dust, the sudden hare which crosses your path, come out of the very set-up of which you are a part, without knowing it, and which drives and precedes you in its advance. *Cras*, says the crow, tomorrow! The birds, arriving, in long flight, from the Sound or from Courland, fling at us, in a far-away cry, news to be pondered, to be discussed, tonight, sullenly, with our fire: (the creation of an "eye"? the moving of a figure on this earth studded with righteous men?) And once upon a time our observation did not go beyond this circle, the narrowest, the one which touches us, the stone on which our foot stumbles when we go out, this man who sneezes at my elbow. But today, we can encompass vaster and richer figures. Each morning, the newspaper gives us a report on the aspect of the earth, the political situation, the stock-exchange. We own the present in its entirety, everything happens before our eyes; the trends of the future appear on the scroll of impressions, which attracts it.

As already stated, the past is the forever-swelled condition of the future, the eternal creative proposition from the tonic to the dominant. Let us break, at last, the chains which have held us in captivity for so long, and trample under our feet the melancholy adage: *the same causes always produce the same effects*. Let us answer first that there is no cause but a total one, that each effect is the varying evaluation of the whole moment, and that each particular cause is but a fiction for our convenience, by means of which we isolate certain premises, by abstracting them in the absolute and endow them with a final existence, in order to bring out an arbitrary minor premise; secondly, and consequently, that causes are never the same, but similar to an operation of growing totals.

I am not going to draw a line under this paragraph: may this discourse emerge in silence and on a blank page! Where only this last question remains unanswered: but, after all, the sense and direction, this *sense and direction* of life we call time, what is it? All movement, we have stated, is *from* and not *toward* a point. There starts the trace. This is the point to which clings all life unfolded by time; it is the string on which the bow starts and ends its play. Time is the means offered to all that which will be to be, in order to be no more. It is the *Invitation to Death* extended to each sentence, to decay in the explanatory and total harmony, to consummate the word of adoration, whispered in the ear of *Sigè*, the Abyss.

Discourse on the Affinity
With the World and
on Oneself

DISCOURSE ON THE AFFINITY * WITH THE WORLD AND ON ONESELF

ARGUMENT

PRELUDE.—Kinship between the words naître and connaître (to come into the world and to know).* On the three types of knowledge.

ARTICLE ONE.—On superficial knowledge, that is, the establishment and discovery of the relationship which exists between things. That which all beings have in common, movement. Wherever there is variety in existence, there is movement. Idea of geometry without space. Nature and we, animated by the same geometrizing power. That which is different for each being, the *end*: or halt to which they are compelled by the other beings. That is, how they get to know the other beings and themselves, by being that which the others lack. All things know each other, by being either adjoining or complementary. Each movement, when reaching its end, results in the creation of equilibrium or form. Thus, two ordinary states of matter, depending on whether it establishes or maintains its balance: efference and vibration. Vibration is movement, prisoner of form. Two kinds of forms: stable and expanding

---

* TRANSLATOR'S NOTE: In Indo-European, the root meaning to know (connaître) was homonymous with that meaning to be born (naître). The author makes use of this double meaning, further combined with that of the Latin "cognatus" (related by blood) in devising the word "co-naître," which will be translated in different ways, according to the context.

forms, that is, forms recorded in duration. Consequently, two elementary kinds of knowledge: knowledge of limits, knowledge of the structure wrought by oneself. How each thing is simultaneously defined and defining: defined by outside things, defining by being outside as compared to them; thus, it knows only that which it excludes by its own existence. Knowledge or effect of oneself, followed in others; the more general a thing, the more generating. Recognition or return of the effect on the cause and discovery of the action suffered.

We do not come into the world alone. To be born for everything, means to be born in affinity with everything, together with. All birth is knowledge (naissance-connaissance).

In order to understand things, we must learn the words which represent, in our mouth, their soluble image. Let us ruminate this intelligible mouthful. The kinship is undeniable between the following ideas in three languages: *to acquire by way of the mind* and *to rise (to appear)*: genîoumai and gignosko, nasci, gignere. novi, cognoscere, naître and connaître (to be born, to know). Everything in the anatomy of these verbs, even the inchoate and passive forms distributed between both families, everything means. Let us interpret: all things recorded in duration are needed by the surrounding structure, preceding their complementary condition and find, outside themselves, the reason for existing, which becomes more perfect in begetting them. Yes, very strictly I call knowledge this necessity for everything to

be a part of something: first. Secondly, this part as the
liberty for man to make, to create, himself, his own position in relation to the whole; and thirdly, this repercus-
sion, which is to know what he is doing.

ARTICLE ONE

Indeed, blue knows orange; indeed, the hand knows
its shadow on the wall; really and truly, the angle of
a triangle knows the other two in the same sense as
Isaac knew Rebecca. All things that are, point, from all
directions, to the ones without which they could not
exist.

This, then, *without which nothing could have been,*
let these words support, for the present, our interpretation of knowledge. First, it is obvious that no part could
exist without the whole, nor all things without each of
them, and, behold, as an example of this interde-
pendence, the human body. There is, among the different organs which make it up, unity of exchange, as
between the heart and the lung, which lives only thanks
to the relationship between themselves; unity of means,
as that established between eye and foot, hand and
mouth; unity of proportions, as the respective weights
of flesh and bones; mere factual unity, as between hair
and toes, simply because they are part of the same individual. All these relations, truly belong to various
orders of knowledge. They really are material and op-

erating elements of knowledge, outside us. Nature
knows with its seas and its mountains, with its mines
and volcanoes and the tiny ends of its sprigs, as we do
with equations, theorems, syllogisms and metaphors.

Therefore, if we define knowledge as the establishment and the discovery of the relations between things,
they should first of all, be able to touch each other, and
be, beyond what each of them does, fundamentally
alike. Alike in what? In *movement* first, or this sense of
direction I have described, attraction and resistance. Out
of the solidarity and support it encounters in its work,
the moving force deducts its *mass* and its *quantity*; out
of the difference between it and other moving forces,
the definitions of distance, dimensions and proportions.
Such are the elements of the mathematical universe,
and the first edition of the Bridge of Asses. All amounts
to the adding of the units, as 2, containing 1, does not re-
quire 3. All necessities are analytical; the lines inscribed
in the folio of sediment, in the muster-roll of the tree,
do not include our complete balance-sheet; an account
is opened for each article, in which, returns and ex-
penses are recorded day by day, and there is only one
necessity, that each balance the others, that each trans-
fer of funds be verified. The cash-register is never
closed, the abacus knows no idleness. If the fundamental aspect of things can be represented by a uniform symbol, inasmuch as submitted to movement
as we represent their exchange and issue-value, in

money form, it is obvious that the whole activity of nature amounts to an arithmetical *operation*, its clearing transfers, from one side to the other, its use in the accounting correspondence. And I do not imagine, like an Epicurean, this preliminary provision of *atoms*, which cannot be different, since they are supposed to be insensible: from the greatest to the smallest, nothing, undoubtedly, appears otherwise than in organic and compound form. This alone is universal and always translated by the solitary and simultaneous unity, according to which all things are subject to movement, to drawing up title deeds, as they are to bed-posts. A figure deserts a total, only to enter another one: addition-subtraction. Like an ear of corn, multiplication is the product of the comparison of a quantity with itself. Everywhere, the conflicting forces perform the partition: the inner sides of a vase are in a position to make the best calculation of the weight of water they enclose; the lid of the earth, like a bar drawn between two numbers, can best appraise the effort of fire, of boiling water, of atmospheric pressure. Each figure is an equation of the unit added to itself, which, as a total represents the Expanse of the various objects making it up, the carrying out of which, constitutes that which is called duration, Time.

At this point, we have to resolve a preliminary doubt.

What are, in relation to each other, the realities represented under the name of matter and spirit? If they are fundamentally heterogeneous, separated down to their very roots, how could they be connected to each other? and know each other, while not knowing each other? We must deny them, therefore, not diversity, which is fertile, but a natural isolation, which is inconceivable. Both are creatures, and depend, thus, on the state of movement.

We have to consider, indeed, that the state of movement is not to be applied solely to bodily things and is not, in any way, synonymous with a local displacement. There is movement wherever there is a variation in existence. An apparition followed by a disappearance constitutes movement, no matter whether these facts are connected to an idea or to a spot on the wall, for instance. These apparitions and these eclipses may constitute a recurrent rhythm, an arithmetical individual, possessing distinct properties. And I even say that, without any space, the ideas of interior and exterior survive, and so do the notions of that which is the thing and that which is not, of that which is the thing, as compared to that which is conditioning it. Whence result immediately the ideas of direction, sense, intention, attention, intension and extension, and their degrees. With the sole idea of its unique existence, the spirit can create all of geometry.

The symbols of geometry, in themselves, do not apply to material dimensions anymore than figures represent stars or cabbage. Both arithmetic and geometry originate in the principle of a unique existence, translated in the latter by a *point*. This point is a pure symbol, independent of any positive outside experience. The possibility of conceiving reality as represented by a point, implies that of conceiving a second identical reality, and so on, and on, indefinitely. This *continuous* possibility, whether actualized or not, is represented by the *line*. The single point provides us with the notion of initiation and beginning. A second point supplies the idea of direction. A series of interdependent points, born from each other, in such a way that it is impossible to get to the last one without passing by all the others, creates the idea of the straight, the parallel, the perpendicular lines. A series of points, each of them separated by an equal number of units from a single starting point, endows us with the idea of the circle and the curve. A number of units, increasing proportionally, adds the idea of angle. Experience supplies us only with paper and ink, so to say, that is the means of representing these ideas, the field on which to project the shadow of our unity.

Far from me the foolish idea that, because our intelligence alone can create geometrical figures and because we see that the entire outside world amounts to these figures, this world be the creation of our intelligence. I only realize that the world and myself are animated by the same geometrizing force that I find equally and easily within or outside myself. So, for instance, when looking at a painting, our eye measures the distance and sets the different planes, establishes the third dimension. We are part of a homogeneous whole, and, as we are connected to all that which is nature, we know it.

But this first article has discussed only the material things, in as far as they know themselves to be ordinary; let us see how they know themselves in their distinguishing traits.

All is movement, or—and the result is the same—all is expressed by it. And movement is, as I have already stated elsewhere, the impossibility for the moving body to subsist, to keep the place it used to occupy; it has a natural tendency to get away, it endeavors to run away. This swerving brings it in contact with the other bodies around it, and leads it to find out what space they leave open to it. Without them, it would be unable to hold the position which belongs to it. They make it possible for it to evaluate the intensity of the work to be achieved, the resistance they offer and the reaction it determines. It provokes or is submitted to their activity. It finds its definition, measure and function outside itself. It knows, that is, it makes use of itself, in order to know that which is not itself, and, inversely, it knows that it is that without which nothing else could be, neither qualitatively, just as no total could exist without each of the component units, nor in its concrete quality, any more than the hour without the wheelwork.

To know, therefore, is to be: that which all the rest lacks.

Nothing is complete in itself; all is drawn from within by itself, from the outside by the vacuum, delineated by its absent form, as each trait is determined by the others. The lake paints on the oval sky the white swan clinging unto it, the bull's eye, the fodder and the shepherd girl. A gust of wind sweeps off, in one blow, the spittle from the sea, the leaf and the bird from the bush, the bonnet from the peasant's head, the smoke from the village and the chimes from the steeple. When dawn comes to life, the vegetable and animal kingdom come out of sleep, like a face slowly overtaken by intelligence. And some ordinary themes are offered to the reflection of various things. The whole surface of the earth and the grass that covers it and the animals that populate it is as sensitive as a plate acted upon by the photographic sun. It is a vast workshop in which everyone endeavors to render the color it takes from the solar hearth.

Things have two means of knowing each other, that is, in the sense adopted in this paragraph, of completing each other in space, by being either contiguous or complementary. They all fit into a more general form, combine into a picture: it belongs to each point of view to look for and find the eyes owing to which they exist. And just as we know things by deciding upon a general characteristic we grant to them, they know each other by taking advantage of a common principle, that is, light similar to a seeing eye. Each of them complies with the necessity of being seen. The rose or the poppy sign in red the bond with the sun, according to which, other flowers are compelled to be white or blue. A certain green could not exist by itself any more than a mass without a prop. Each note of a scale calls for and implies the others. None of them aspires to satisfy the feelings all by itself. It exists on condition that it should not sound like the others, but also on the imperative condition that the others should sound as it does not. There is knowledge of each other, obligation between them, thus relationship between the various parts of the world, as between the parts of speech, so that they may constitute a readable sentence; and, similarly, there is a consistency in sentiments, as in the words expressing them; and movements follow a pattern, as proven by hours. The wheelwork manufacturing it could not stop any more than time itself. Movement is not a temporary state of matter, local and accidental; it is not a mere property, a "force" which cannot be separated from matter; it is its permanent act, and the very instrument of its existence. Weight is not the result of an "attraction" exerted from the outside on an otherwise inert mass. The mass itself contains its own impetus and the stone flies toward the earth like a bird toward a tree.

All movement results in the creation or maintenance of a state of equilibrium. In the field of matter, organized or unorganized, this equilibrium is to be found only in the establishment of a combination form or figure. All

that which is, strives toward being more completely;
that is, toward constructing the idea in which it can
take pleasure in its organic differences. These forms
have in themselves a permanent, absolute and compulsory value, a mechanical requirement, and a necessity
of display. They are truly bodies, and all things are
embodied in them.

Consequently, two common states of matter, depending on its establishing or maintaining the equilibrium;
efference and vibration. The first, according to the point
of view, corresponds quite well to the words standing in
our mind for conception and imagination. Or, rather, it
is their present, but accidental and fleeting expression, a
demolished structure about to be reconstructed. Matter
could not even exist without a series of more and more
general and almost concentric forms in which it settles
and organizes. The second state is the ascertainment of
the degree of order it has reached. Nothing in nature is
subject to inertia. The marble, in which the sculptor
tries to imitate it, is as much alive as the arm with which
Hercules holds his monster; and were it not for the
strength of the common effort accomplished by the vast
combination of muscles and bones constituting the body
of the earth, they would no more succeed in holding it
in place than the cleverly tied up webs of our stomach
in keeping our bowels together without the accuracy of
our nervous battery. Vibration is movement held in
check by form. This vibration is expressed, according to

environment, in a certain order, which is upset by any outside contact or shock: this is the first stage of sensitivity.

Forms, as we have defined them, that is compound places or figures, do not imply rest, but they perpetually integrate the action they are supposed to be: to become, to subsist. Two kinds of forms can be discerned, and, likewise, two types of formations. The first is an entity in itself, and safely guarded and protected against any influence from the outside, which would destroy its balance, does not necessarily imply any change. The chemical substances are manufactured once and for all and a rectangular triangle is perfectly defined, except for its revolution around one of its sides. The second type includes a series of successive stages, solidarily and necessarily linked together, so that any stoppage in their production leads to the disappearance of the form itself. This *mode* is called development. We no longer witness the sudden substitution of one form for another, as in the transposition of equivalents in chemistry: matter suffering passively the contacts forced upon it. Here, form moulds and creates itself. The tree in the soil, man in his mother's womb have a sound knowledge of self beforehand. Development is form recorded in duration, as elsewhere on the plane of the surface, and its successive parts are as solidary as simultaneous limbs. The germ knows all it has to do, it fulfills its task in each detail; it chooses, in its surroundings,

the food it needs, as an artist, his colors, as a brick-
layer, his bricks and his mortar. The tricks of Scapin,
the involved plot of melodramas, the ingenuity dis-
played by Columbine and Harlequin to be together in
spite of the interference of jealousy are trifles, when
compared with the cunning devised by the parasite to
reach his maturity, through three or four different or-
ganisms. The first stage, as I have already stated, of the
knowledge a body acquires about itself is the realization
of the place it occupies, that is, of the impossibility to
back out of the setting of which it is a part: the vibration, or shock, followed by a multiple recurrence, is the
first inner feeling. We are now considering the second
stage, external and active; in the image created by a
living being, in the structure it erects around itself, it no
longer exists through a mere limitation, opposed from
the outside; it comes into being from within.

Going back to our principle: *to know is to establish
that without which the rest could not be,* we discover
that knowledge consists of various degrees of precision
and necessity. There is one absolute necessity: *the
whole could not exist without its parts.* There are concrete and secondary necessities or expediencies, depending on whether the being itself or the designated being
is involved. There is no end but that which, by ending,
excludes the ended exterior, and knowledge varies with
contact. Each body constitutes the final term of a com-

bination of converging series, its common, final and absolutely necessary result. Several such series are in constant contact with the body, so that it could not even exist without their preliminary or simultaneous appearance; others, a purely accidental, nonetheless necessary contact, since it contributes to its definition, to the determination of its point in duration. Just as one color is limited by another color, so does the body designate, from all sides around it, the last terms, constant or not, of sequences, originating in infinity. It supports, stops and coordinates them; it ties up, it is the infinitely complex intersection of the yarn with the woof. To define a thing means literally to fix its limits by means of the permanent or fleeting elements of the well determined space in which it is set. Thus, all things are defined and defining; they are defined in all their points, they define by one only. A thing knows through that which it excludes, in fact or by nature. It is surrounded by the radiations of its clues. To define, is to isolate, to exclude: it means stating why a thing is not all the others. When two terms are in opposition each of them adds to the total of differences which constitute the other. The formula would be more or less the following: "This thing is not that one, of which I am a part; it does not exhaust that which exists; my existence alone prevents it from integrating the total and I make it richer by adding myself to all the things it is not; I am invested with the right of denying it totality while finding in it the point which makes mine impossible."

Knowing only that which it excludes, each thing knows only that which it is not and that which is not itself.

And so, it can very well be said: to be, is not to be a thing, it is not to be any other, it is to be prevented from being it, either by a material opposition or by its needing me as I am. Knowledge is the realization of my boundaries.—But there is knowledge, and there is acknowledgment, depending on whether a thing is considered as cause or being caused.

(*Cause:* means supplied to a thing to be or to look what it is. The cause of heat, the Cause of Justice).

Knowledge, therefore, considered here only in its *real* sense of causation and action exerted on the outside world, is the effect of oneself, traced on others. This effect or result is expressed either by a mere impossibility for the other to occupy the place I occupy, or by an impulse, a work accomplished of which I am the source and the other the subject. This knowledge may take the name of information, since its aim is the creation of a form. It is in this sense that the sea knows the boat; the axe and its native rock, both know the oak; the fire, the food it cooks, the metal it melts. Rome it sets ablaze. The farther action goes from its source, so far goes knowledge. You must understand that the more *general* a thing, the more *generating* it is. A thing is established or defined by all its actions, limited in fact, unlimited in possibilities, like the number of things that can come within its scope.

Acknowledgment is the converse of this first term. One gives and the other requests. One proposes, the other disposes. One proves and the other experiences. It accepts moderately, from that which surrounds it, opposition, impulsion or nourishment. Accident or necessity, fleeting or permanent, encounter or coupling. The second term receives from the first a contrast to establish, an energy to convert, a force to handle. While the latent activities of rough matter wait for the opportunity to escape or for the subject through which to manifest themselves, like smoke in a sun-ray, the plant and the animal are constantly active; out of the food they obtain, they manufacture their own existence: their life is but their compliance with the source from which they draw it. *Acknowledgment* requires *knowledge* as a prerequisite, for knowledge brings it forth. The second term can not exist without the first, but the contrary is not true. Soil is always fertile, no matter what the crop; straw or books, both are equally welcome to the fire which consumes them; grass nourishes all the various animals which live on it. But roses cannot exist without a special type of soil nor insects without a special kind of fruit. Cause can exist without its effect, but not effect without cause. The latter is, for the first, a means of being among others; the first is the very reason of the other's existence. The "known" one knows only itself, and the means without which it could not exist as such; the "acknowedged" knows another thing without which it could not be and which defines it accurately. Of course, this differentiation is only logical, since both qualities can meet in the same subject.

These principles are established.

ARTICLE TWO

ARGUMENT

ARTICLE TWO.—On knowledge in the Living. The vital act is, above all, the elaboration of the nervous vibration. About sensation being an active and not a passive condition of the being.—The vegetable, or elaboration of the combustible matter. The animal or the condition of ignited matter providing for its own living. Respiration or the balance between the needs of the individual and the requirements from the outside. On the essential vital vibration, or movement, which proceeds from a center and reaches the points of an area circumscribed within the bounds it sets when ceasing. Two moments of vibration, emission and reaction. All vibration reaches and occupies a form. All forms are closed. Our nervous system is consecrated to the elaboration of vibration. It is that which quivers in contact with Being. Our being is born every minute and contacts other bodies, thus getting to know them. The palpable knowledge of man is a conscious birth, qualified by the object which limits its expansion. To know by means of the senses, is to create oneself insofar as qualified

by a certain sensation. On an apparatus dedicated to our contact with the outside world. On feeling. On taste. On smell.
On sight. Digression: justification of "anthropomorphism." On
our manufacturing ourselves the energy with which the optical
waves from the outside harmonize. On hearing or the direct
sense of movement and duration. Wherever he be, man *knows*,
assembles different things within himself.

I have indicated in the preceding pages that, outside ourselves, there is a knowledge things have of each
other, according to the relationship they maintain.
Analysing the word, I found ideas of combination and
production, of form and movement. I portrayed the
figure of Pan, the passion of the universe, tormented by
the impossibility of subsisting. I defined the notion of
part, each being indispensable to the other and to all.
I have said enough about the *knowledge of construction:* I shall now talk about the *knowledge of finding
out,* as devolving upon our mind.

By applying the principles acquired, I understand
that, for man as well as for other beings, to live is to
know. What then is the particular mode of his knowledge of life?

The vital, essential act of the human being is the
elaboration of the nervous vibration.

In order to make myself understood, I am reproducing here the lines laid down in the pages of another
book, "Sur la Cervelle."

"The brain is an organ. The student acquires sound

principles if he firmly grasps the thought that the nervous system is homogeneous in its nucleus and its ramifications, and that its function is merely as determined by its mechanical efficiency. There is nothing to justify the excesses attributed to the white or grey substance, in addition to the sensitive and motor function of 'secreting,' as the noise made by a semblance of words, intelligence and will, in the same way as liver produces bile. The brain is an organ in its own right just as the stomach and the heart; and, as the digestive or the circulatory system have their well defined functions, so does the nervous system; its function being to produce sensation and movement.

"I used the word 'to produce' purposely. It would be an error to consider the nerves as mere threads, mere agents—inert as individual entities—of a double transmission, afferent—as it is called—here, efferent, there; equally willing to wire a noise, a shock, or the order of the inner spirit. The system controls the maturing of the cerebral wave, constant like the pulse, and its spreading all over the body. Sensation is not a passive phenomenon; it is a special state of action. I am comparing it to a vibrating string, on which the note is formed by the correct position of the finger. Through sensation I realize the fact, and through movement, I control the act. But vibration is constant.

"And this point of view enables us to proceed with our investigation. Every vibration implies a source, as each implies a center. Nervous vibration originates in the brain, which, independent of all other organs, fills the entire cavity of the hermetically closed skull. The rule of analogy quoted in the first line prevents us from considering it as something else than the receiving transformation and, to a certain extent, a digestive agent of the initial commotion. One can imagine this role to be especially devised for the peripheric substance, which is formed by the white substratum, a kind of amplifying and composition agent; and, finally, one can also imagine the complicated organs, underlying the whole, to be, each and everyone, carrying-out shops, distribution-boards, key-boards and meters, switches and timing apparatus.

"We shall now consider vibration itself: I mean, the double and unique movement which removes a body from one point and takes it back again. And therein lies the very 'element,' the radical symbol which is essentially life. Our brain's vibration is the effervescence of the source of life, the emotion of matter in contact with the divine unity, whose influence constitutes our typical personality. Such is the navel of our dependence. The nerves and the contact we establish with the outside world, are but the instrument of our knowledge and, only in this sense, do they condition it. We educate our senses, according to the same method used in learning everything about a tool. We learn the world by learning about our intimate identity.

"The brain is, thus, merely an organ: the organ of animal knowledge which takes the form of sensations in animals, and becomes intelligible, in man. But, since it is just an organ—be it even a special one—it cannot be the support of intelligence and of the soul. No part of our body, living and active image of any God, should be abused in this way. The human soul is that through which the human body is what it is, its act, its continually active seed, and, according to the pronouncement of Scholars, its form."

The life of the planet is essentially acquired; its way of being is to grow or to perish. This growth is a storing of the substance it draws from the earth through its roots, from the air, through its breathing leaves; its force is controlled by this double influence, its living *capacity* by the countenance expressed in its form. The substance it acquires, that which it prepares and completes in dying, by returning the water it has consumed, amounts to this: enough to be burned and dissolved by this flame whose living image it is.

If the vegetable can be defined as "the combustible substance," the animal is burning substance. In the former, the form or quality is equivalent to the quantity of substance it contains and accumulates. But the living body, soon reaching maturity and stripped of its first clothes,—apprenticeship or disguise necessary to cover the germinal spark—remains alive only by destroying itself and by thus feeding itself out of itself. It is an instrument of consumption; it must convert the nourishment taken from the outside to feed its own hearth by working it in a closed vessel. This digestion, this necessary destruction, implies the isolation of the subject, its separation—measured in terms of need—from the source of supply, a spontaneous striving at starting anew. In growing, the vegetable fills the form assigned to it; the animal maintains its form by burning whatever it needs to satisfy the hunger for fire concealed in it. The living body, being unable to grow, maintains its form only by eliminating the surplus substance. It lives only by destroying itself. Like the clock and the hour-glass, it functions by the dropping of the disintegrating substance within itself. Separated from the aperture which fixed it to its Creator, it is caught by the sea of movement into which it plunges, inhales its impulse in even the remotest parts of its body, and, after receiving additional air, it restores its decayed organs. The effect of this or any other fire is the destruction of a libratory arrangement, the elements of which, searching, in the state of efference, their affinity groups, split, according to their interior impetus, into force and residue.

The animated being is hollow; like a bottle, it bears witness to the breath which has formed it and which reinflates it with each one of its aspirations. This vacuum consists of a state of native disequilibrium, an internal and passive demolition, compensated by an active re-

trieval from the outside. We have imagined that all
form is the work and the proof of a certain vibratory
swinging; enclosed in the so called inert matter, in the
form of a recurrent cycle, vibration is the scale on which
a body eternally weighs each one of its parts; (I have explained elsewhere the meaning I give to the word
weight). The vital system manifests, amplifies this eco-
nomical oscillation, which stands at the intersection,
between the needs of the individual and the outside
requirements which encumber it; the vital section is the
elective action within us, it is the feed-box and the trap.
Let us examine our human vibration and discover its
source and its activity.

The vibration through which we realize the existence
and the limitations of our person is the same one which
has created and continues to maintain it. The essential
creative act is the emission of a wave. The wave can be
tentatively defined as a movement which originates in
a center and reaches all the points of an area circumscribed by the bounds it draws when completed. It
determines, in each of these points, a local displacement, followed by a reaction, or tendency to come back
to the first spot; the surmounting of this tendency requires the accumulation of a new effort, the impulse of
a second wave. Thus, two movements, one eccentric
from the motor the other concentric as compared with
the subject, the two *moments* of the vibration. The
effect of the wave is an *internal formation* or extension

of a certain form within the area it determines. Form is nothing but a variation of the circle. By form, I mean, not only the outline of a certain figure, but, owing to its being closed, the constitution of a certain medium, in as much as all its parts obey the rhythm which regulates them. The stroke of a mallet on a drum produces a sonorous existence. Light and heat are the effects of impulses originating in the womb of matter. I propose these simple images. But it is also an infinitely complex and varied vibration, a vibration provided with willpower, as proven by its ultimate frolics, this vortex at the tips of our fingers and the star of hair on the top of our head. Just as a note is formed on an instrument, and a song out of a group of chosen notes, so also, in the mother's womb, is the infant endowed with a face and an echoing soul.

The cerebral and nervous substance, the cranial and spinal marrow with its elements so free,—similar to stars with their retractile rays, to notes which would play themselves, stretching their fingers in all directions,—is the source and the workshop of these creative vibrations, of the sacred original shudder. This essential repulsion, *this necessity of not being* That, gives us life, and, by being something else, it warps our substance, inspires and puts us together. We live only to resist, to start the mysterious struggle of Israel all over again. We do not lose contact. We have within ourselves something which does not cease shivering; we do not cease being

placed on the source; we have within ourselves, the key
and the recording meter. In the angular stone of our
bones, in the case of our stem our movement lies concealed, like the spring in the barrel. It is this movement
which makes us walk; it controls the escapement, the
consumption of each of our organs. We can proportion
its intensity, localize its action, so as to determine the
displacement of the various parts of our body. We are
free to resort to the source we carry within ourselves;
like a pump which can draw, in one suction, just such
a volume of water and no more; closely related to the
force which repels the worlds, we are capable of drawing the supply of energy we use, according to our needs,
and manage, according to our whim.

Everything being thus defined, we can now consider
man as a body in a permanent state of vibration, or, to
use terms we have found to be congeneric, of beginning
and information. But this body is surrounded by other
bodies; it does not come to life by itself; at each moment
of its duration, it is *born together with*. In this primitive
meaning, it completes—like all bodies—the general unity
in which it appears, it fills a compartment, it is the converse of the other bodies which determine its presence,
its production, its place in the space they occupy jointly.
Such is the first position; by an object's position, we
mean that it is vertical or oblique, on the right or the
wrong side. A stone in the hands of one who knows the
right questions, a piece of floating wood, the insect on

which I throw my hat give an answer and do not keep silent. And, I ask, will man, by his sole presence, have less explanatory value than all these? Isn't there an adjustment, right and left? Isn't his person involved in a less copious and varied story? Is it not his duty to give accounts? He practices knowledge. Let us see in what particular mode.

We have said that all things amount to the establishment of a certain equilibrium or vibration. I have defined knowledge as the relationship each one maintains with the others, because of the resistance it offers, the action it exerts and the reaction it suffers. No object has been created once and for all; it does not stop being created; it is continually produced, it expresses the state of permanent tension of the effort whose expression it is. Consequently, the principle of its existence and form is also the instrument of its knowledge. The knowledge of man can be defined as a conscious birth, *qualified by the thing which limits its expansion.* If we imagine the field of animal vibrations schematically, as a circle, whose ultimate wave is the circumference, we can represent all sensations coming from the outside, by an indentation which is of interest not only to the external form, but to the entire surface of the area it circumscribes. Each wave, proceeding from the center is inflected by this obstacle; the entire subject takes on a special *internal form* (*information*). Each vital emission reproduces the first one: each of them retrieves the conquered field in its entirety, by growing, reloads man, strains once more the nerves of the machine which set it up, verifies all that which is included within the limits of the individual it has created. It teaches me that I am and what I am by means of that which I am not. I am, meaning that I am not the various things which surround me; I am in as much as I am limited by them, in as much as I feel this limitation, in as much as I am informed by it, in as much as I feel its influence on me; I am endowed with seeing and hearing; I see, I taste, I smell this fire, this fruit, this rose.

Thus, while we recreate our own existence, we create it as modified by the external influences which surround us. We are the authors of our sensations; between us and them there is a cause and effect relationship, meaning that, owing to the intervention of an extraneous medium and of the body against which we are squeezed, we are determined within them, ad quid, we create ourselves in such or such a state of sensitivity. That which creates us is the very thing which gives us knowledge.

There is no means or need here for more particulars. We can however see that, like emission, the preparation, tension and *intention* of the nervous wave is the achievement of the central organs and that the cerebro-medullary system is nothing but a laboratory of movement. This movement keeps in good shape the various devices which, on the surface of the body, control our contact with the outside, being in charge of what I would call the *digestion of the shock*.

Some of these devices supply only local information to the subject and partial information to the object; the others provide a complete image.

Among the first group, the simplest is that of touch. Our skin is naked; we are sensitive in all points of our form, we are equal to our envelope. Contact is a mere action on the circuit, painful if it disturbs or interrupts it, agreeable, sometimes, if it accelerates it. Such is the purely passive touch, but our hands play an active part, which can be transferred wherever we want. They are not meant merely to appraise the soft and the resistant, the rough and the smooth. They are, at the extremity of our arm, a metric reduction of ourselves. They give us the first measure—I refer to the effort corresponding to the sample of sensitivity ·they discover. The *rule o'thumb*, the touch of our four fingers on the thumb provides us with our tool for numbers and surfaces. The articulated angle of our phalanxes, the opening of the various compasses with which we are equipped, acquaint us with the sphere and volume.

Touch in itself provides us only with partial informations; it is merely a part of our body in contact with such and such a part of another; the four other senses supply us with general informations, vested in a special and isolated organ. Through the mouth and the nose, I obtain (I and not my mouth or my nose, directly and without any deductive operations) informations on everything by which a piece of meat or a grain of musk is flavor or perfume. Taste is but a more complete touch, a compenetration made possible by the pressure of the jaws, the cooking and the hot oven of the mouth with its jets of saliva which dissolve and dilute the food masticated by our molars. The nose is the funnel through which we draw the air into ourselves, judging the fumes and spirits. Smell always indicates a decomposition, whether due to heat or humidity, an efference, an expansion reciprocal to that of our lungs which open to inhale, and make life out of that breath, purified in passing through the filter of the incoming passage. Mythology shows us the gods fed by the smoke of sacrifices.

The two higher senses do not give merely impressions; but each of them, on different levels, images.

We have, deep inside ourselves, an obstinately prehensile truth, in spite of the cry of the Ape-tree, clamoring the horrible Greek word "anthropomorphism," namely that man, a conscious portion of a homogeneous activity, legitimately draws inferences about the external world on the basis of his own nature; that he carries within himself the roots of all the forces which operate the world, of which he is the abridged version and the didactic document. To understand is to be in communion, to join the fact with its keys, which are in our possession. I know everything by heart before opening my eyes, and this black art, comprised within myself, does not demand less of the skies, when I open them, than the sun I find there, established in fact. I understand what it is doing there. I am, just like the sun, a source of light and energy. And the light wave, in its expansion, does not meet any inert bodies, but, everywhere, more or less compact or complicated power systems in operation. It is compelled to take this obstacle into account, to modify its rhythm and pace accordingly. This reaction, this ignition of the object due to the solar shock is what we call color. I use the word ignition purposely, for this illumination, this coloring of the object constitutes a special state of its vibratory function, in the same sense as combustion. Commotion and not destruction, color is the herald of flame. Let us take a circle having the source of light as its center. Since the propagation of light takes place in a straight line, we can consider each point of the circumference as being connected to the center by the "ray," this word taken in its double, optical and geometrical, meaning. Let us now study the animal eye. The membrane called "retina," which lines its back is an apparatus of intense vibratory elaboration. Its miscroscopic figuration shows that it is both a battery and a "loom," a battery composed of two elements of unequal length, one blunt, the other sharp, the "cones" and the "rods." We can therefore consider the eye as a kind of portable, miniature sun, endowed, like its prototype with the faculty of sending out "rays" to connect it with each point on the circumference. Just as the sonorous wave in the telephone uses the vehicle created by the electric current, so the eye clings to light. It is built to correspond to its rhythm, either the free one or that which, breaking on an extraneous body, produces color. The shock, which, at one end of the ray produces color, determines, upon returning, on the back of our eye, sensation, owing to its impact on the workshop which is about to weave its flash. Sight does not result from an image represented on our brain, but from a real contact with the object touched and circumscribed by our eyes. Similar to a rigid system, the ray reproduces, at one end, the movement which affects the other.

While the other senses give us impressions in succession, sight homologates contrasting and simultaneous ones. Soon we learn to recognize these groups, these associations of colors we call images and the indentation they cause—owing to the play of our pair of eyes—and to distinguish them from the background where they are fitted together. We perceive them at once and prepare a different way of looking for each of them. The perception of a tree or a wall corresponds to such or such a state of my sensitivity; I make my gaze at this wall and this tree; I make this tree and this wall within myself.

Sight gives us images of space; hearing draws their duration. One of these images is built on difference and the other one on variation. One molds itself, the other modulates itself. The wall and the very foundation of our skull is pierced through on each side. We listen, that is, we lend ourselves to the sound which invades and penetrates us. The organ of hearing with its fossae, its circuits and its canals, the thousands of filaments, immersed into a moving liquid, could not be compared more adequately than to that of digestion. A sort of concha and echo are inserted into our skull. Any scream draws an answer from us and strikes our tympanum on the taut membrane which occludes its aperture. And the auditive process is a sort of distillation of the sonorous wave, separating each of the constitutive elements of noise, so as to reintegrate them in the form of sensation. As the nose inhales odors, the ear appreciates sound according to the way it *passes*; it mounts the scale of organs meant to compute its vibrations.

The sense of hearing is, indeed, essentially the sense of that which goes on, of the pitch of sounds, the shrill, the flat being merely the indication of their speed. The sonorous waves have the characteristic of being slow enough to permit our perceiving and counting their throbs; they are infinitely variable in intensity, in composition, in the speed of their successive variations; they are never continuous in their emission; finally, this emission can always be attributed to well determined and special causes. The variety of forms and colors is due to that of the things which happen to be exposed to daylight, enduring in solid light, the vibratory medium having no other function than that of transmitting them to us. On the contrary, in the case of sound, vibration itself is produced and becomes the object of our knowledge and our criticism. It can be said that sound is both the portrait of movement and its image, abstract and sensitive at the same time. The person auditively informed becomes sound, that is, modified by sound, just as, in the alternative of sight, it becomes color, that is, modified by color in its vibratory roots. Thus, it becomes the instrument of pure movement and of time on the march. But we have stated above that movement is the very act, the expressive condition, the meaning of all things. Movement is never uniform; it has always its crisis and its periods. Thus, sound is essentially that which begins and ceases, that which traces the phase from one end to the other. Ear is the instrument thanks to which man can appreciate all the rhythms and aspects of the movement which animates him, using its own flow as a continuous basis. Man is free to create the sonorous image of this pace of life; and this is the origin of music and speech. I am just pointing out the premises, the consequences of which I shall subsequently develop.

I have finished all I had to say on sensitive knowledge. For a long time to come, we will, undoubtedly, be unable to go any further, to trace sensation back to its source to the distribution board, to this central station where the wave feeding the various peripheric organs receives its first impulse. The same nervous pulsation which is responsible for our sight, enables us to smell and to hear, when guided on different networks. Our sensory organs are but apparatus for the transformation of the initial current, and, so to say, ignition apparatus constructed for various switches. Consequently, they are interdependent and the pressure which produces sight, for instance, requires the same expansion of the circumference limited elsewhere by sound, and thus our eyes can recognize noise.

On the other hand, if we consider that movement and sensation have a common origin, we can perceive, in this double order of activity, the total means for man to attain and to realize the limits of the place assigned to him. He constitutes, himself, wherever he may be, a center, and he enjoys the privilege of transporting this center wherever he pleases. Just as a piece of gold or of coal is the symbol of the many forces which have produced and conserved it, so man, by reason of his existence *here,* becomes the coordinating point of the various phenomena to which he bears witness. He explains them, he finds the relationship between them, he knows them by merely being present. If a wretched pebble accounts for the whole universe, how much more the sensitive animal which was the subject of this second article. We shall presently speak about the rational and intelligent animal.

ARTICLE THREE

ARGUMENT

ARTICLE THREE.—On intellectual knowledge and, first of all, on general ideas. On constancy. Constancy is the characteristic of all closed forms and the result of a continuous effort. Similarly, the sensation or form qualified from the outside is constant. The constant sensation of a constant thing is the basis of our general ideas. I call general the quality that various things have in common, and which is, consequently, due in both cases to the same action. The most general and only universal quality is movement. To know the similar is to be connected. Uniformity of chemical reactions. Uniformity of animal reactions. The sensations producing movement and action; the animal is uniformly connected to the object to which it is suited and which will extend a uniform invitation in this sense. The animal has a particular reason for existing, man has a general reason for existing, namely reason itself. He is master of his connections, he is made to be at ease everywhere. He knows the general everywhere, and may thus be placed in a state of relationship in which he excels. We know things by supplying them with a means of exerting an action on our movement, we produce them in as much as they are connected with us, we are masters of a generating sensation and of its abstract reduction by the abridged effect which is its image, that is the general idea. On memory and the faculty of repeating series of generating and interlinked efforts. On symbols and images. On the man-made symbol or word. The word *calls forth*, provokes, within us, the state of connection which cor-

73

responds to the sensitive presence of the things themselves. The words illustrate either our personal state of tension, or this state as informed by objects. *Knowledge*: or realization of the general figure, according to which we are apt to establish connections. *Intelligence*: or repetition, within us, of the word which calls each object into being in connection with us.

Before discussing the subject of general ideas, let us settle the notion of constancy.

The constant in all things is the closed form under which it exists. As we have seen, everywhere, in rough as in organized matter, form is not the result of cutting out a pattern once and for all, but the product of a constant operation which maintains it. If form be constant, so is the effort which constitutes it. In the case of a sensitive animal, *form* can be defined as the quantity of matter limited by contact. By contact, I mean the pressure exerted from the outside on all the senses. The same operation of nervous elaboration which insures the maintainance of its form, is used by the animal for the upkeep of its contact. The form is constant and so is the sensation. Constant also that which maintains it, as such, or that which limits its from within as well as from without. Sensation is not only constant, it is also unique in its original source, which is nervous pulsation; the latter is different only according to the apparatus which canalises and predisposes it. Each sensation is unique since it is the product of the same current supplied by the central switch and diversified because of the various obstacles which stop and interrupt it. It would therefore seem that, figuratively speaking, a special and well determined section of the rays we dart from all our senses corresponds to each of these obstacles. Thus, we shall henceforth consider each of these objects as tantamount to a special way of being interrupted by this section; this interruption will be its image, in other terms, a *sensation*. The same object will always produce the same sensation and any variation of one will be reciprocally translated by the other. So, for example, a tree: any tree produces, on each of our senses, a category of never varying impressions, accompanied by other more or less special ones which define the species and the individual. A constant object produces a constant sensation, and all more or less constant variations of this object, an accordingly more or less constant sensation. The constant sensation of a constant object: this is the basis of our general ideas. Now, we have to discuss the possibility of comparing our isolated experiences and of declaring them similar or different.

But let us first explain the word general which arises at this point, and, in order to do this, let us go back to the first pages of the preceding thesis.[1] I call "general," the quality in which different things are common, that is as if they were one. If two otherwise different things display a similar quality, it is obvious that they do not

[1] Knowledge of Time,—I. *On Cause.*

owe it to themselves, but to a third thing, which is general, that is, as far as they are concerned, it generates this quality, *una in diversis*. The more general this third term, that is the more numerous and varied the cases to which it fits, the more remote the effects it causes, and the richer the possibilities the subject offers to a number of varied means, the more widespread also, its generating power. Thus, the general is the property common to several different things; the most general that which makes the greatest number of different things alike; and the absolutely general, that which makes all things, without any exception, alike. Only one such universal property exists, and that is movement. But then, how do we estimate in what respect the outside things and the corresponding sensations within us are alike or different?

Each sensation is a birth; each birth is a simultaneous birth-knowledge. The animated being knows that which is alike, because it affects it in like way.

But in this sense, what is the difference between man and the other animals?

We witness all substances, in chemistry, reacting in a constant and well determined manner, in presence of a given salt or acid. And so do the delicate organic compounds elaborated by vegetables, and the vegetable specimens themselves, under the influence, for example, of day and night. But the animals, in turn, constitute as sound, but much more subtle and minute a comment on the external action exerted on them. Their conditions of life are more numerous, their needs greater, their chemical balance more sensitive, their mechanism more precise and more complicated. They put more principles into play in order to use more powers. The characteristic of animals is movement; they can therefore be considered as engines created in view of a given movement. We can judge barbs or horses from Perche, reptiles and apes as we do wheelbarrows and bicycles and infer their functioning from their parts. The animal is created to fit into certain specific living conditions; life subjects its maintenance and reproduction to the performing of certain special movements. Just as the circle or polygon is inserted into a plane, according to its shape, so, the animal controls, in nature, its animated form. It knows and becomes related to things according to certain stipulated conditions, the ox, according to the grass it grazes; a scarabaeus, according to the cherry or apricot pit, perforated by its larva. Among the outside objects, some affect its specific form, some do not. In the first case, the object causes the sensation and the sensation, in turn, its movement and its effects, or place. So, a constant object produces a constant sensation, which, in turn, produces the movements necessary to the maintenance of a constant form. The sensations are considered effective or not, depending on whether they are likely to bring about movement or not, that is to make known an object according to which the subject is liable to be related or not. Similar sensations being indicative of a similar object, constitute an invitation to similar movements to reach this object. The form of the animal is the very one under which its sensations are classified as *general,* in relation to the animal, that is, as liable to maintain, to limit it from the outside, and—from the inside—to reintegrate it. The animal is constructed so as to fit into certain surroundings. We can say that it is sensitive—in a certain way—as we say that a compass, a barometer, or a photographic plate is *sensitive,* according to the degree of finesse and accuracy with which these instruments record the external actions for which they are set.

But man is born to "fit" anywhere.

The only constancy is that of form. To maintain a constant form, a constant operation. The nature of a polygon is determined by the number of its sides, the general or motive sensations of the animal, which can be called *apprehensive,* are adapted to a small number of external invitations to which it responds with an infallible and mechanical faithfulness. On the contrary, man is able to adapt himself anywhere, to achieve his form in relationship to any thing, by being different, to be simultaneously born and related according to anything. All sensations, as related to him, being liable to be generative, that is, general, he can take his apprehension anywhere, indiscriminately. He must therefore be free to choose the object causing it. Because of the infinite complexity of the combinations of which he is a part, he must master his sensitive and motive knowledge. In a word, the animal has a particular reason for existing, man has an absolute reason for being, that is just Reason; he controls, he directs, he exploits the force which creates him. In the animal, *sense* alone is apprehensive, sense, that is the instinct of deciding on the direction it must choose in order to agree with circumstances; but man is guided by reason.

So, in contrast with the animal, which is a special being, man is a general one, the first, adapted to special conditions, the latter, to general conditions; one contacts according to the special, the other, according to the general; the animal knows the special, man is simultaneously born according to and knows the general. The dog is led by the nose, the ox has merely to lower his head in order to graze, the monkey to close his four hands on the branches of the tree he inhabits, a certain fruit, a certain soil, even a certain moment, although outside influences, are as absolutely necessary to a type of existence as the anatomic details they control. The animal offers a ready-made series of releases to predetermined keys. But man has been created so as to be in agreement with everything. Therefore, he must possess the means of being modified in his form by everything, to be inwardly molded or informed by everything. But this common element—that he must find in everything —capable of molding him inwardly or of informing him can only be the most general, that is, movement itself, by which all exists.

We have seen that, in animals, the difference between the sensations we called general (or generating) and all the others lies in the fact that the first are effective, that is, followed by the special effect necessary to the maintenance of form. In this case, there is apprehension from the subject, tension of energy toward the apprehended object, attention and intention, contribution of the mechanism to the external key, capable of operating the click (I am deliberately over-simplifying). Likewise in man the transition from sensation to movement, the consciousness of the place to maintain and of the means to hold it are often achieved as by themselves and without any special intervention of willpower; the heat and the expansion of the skin pores, a tickling and the gesture of the hand, in the direction of the irritated spot. But we have said that man must find his place in the midst of everything, that, consequently, he must be able to make life out of everything, to be informed by everything, and thus be capable of discerning in everything—so as to cling to it—the general and common quality which supplies him with this information; in a word, that he is capable of choice and abstraction. For this purpose, he is endowed with a special tool, the vibratory impulse by which he exists and which he can guide at will. Owing to the various senses with which he is endowed, he can press it, like a finger on the objects around him, register on it the constant modification they cause, infer by the constancy of the external action the one which conditions their intrinsic constitution and thus recognize the general in them.

We have attributed to the animal's general sensation the characteristic of always producing the same effect on the position it is destined to hold. The same action produces the same figure. The same is true of man. But just as sensation in him attains what is absolutely general, that is, generating, in the object, in like manner it acts on that which is absolutely generating in him. It does not determine him, it *charges* him, it puts him in a position to determine himself; it gives him the power to act. Indeed, being made to fit anywhere, to invent a common *reason* for infinitely remote and multiple terms, his movement, like his apprehension, in a word, his *sense and direction* must be regulated by a choice, a process of abstraction. I must be informed in order to select satisfactorily the conditions surrounding me; I must establish contacts, according to them.

In short, we know things by supplying them with a means of exerting an action on our "movement." We establish a relationship, we produce them in their relations with us. To shake a hand means to produce myself shaking a hand; to smell a rose means to produce myself smelling that rose. This sensation *generates* an I smelling the rose and this rose as it appears to my senses. This sensation is general, in as much as the same object stops me, confines me at the same point, and thus determines the same form, the same sensation. I substitute for the limit and for the effect, which, in the figure of things is thrust upon the operation which produces them, the reciprocal limit and effect which, in my sensation of them, is thrust upon the operation which produces me. Thus, I perceive them as engendered, that is as general, as the constant effect of the constant cause of the same force, the measure and principle of which are embedded in me; I feel upon my own resilience the decision which determines their form. I am as conscious of the term limiting me—whether it be the same one or a different one—as I am of the movement which conditions me, as will be seen in the next article.

Raw materials, organic compounds, living tissues are, by virtue of their own nature, sensitive to certain actions determined beforehand. Similarly, animated beings are advised by the pleasure or pain they experience of that which agrees or disagrees with them. The series of painful or agreeable, good or wrong, of effort or ease establish themselves, without any outside help, from object to subject and from sensation to movement. Just as a well determined order exists between the different states the individual is bound to produce in succession, in order to achieve the stretching and use of the limbs and instruments with which he is provided, so also between the sensations he procures for himself through his various connections with the outside. The series begun in-

side requires, implies its last terms, the necessary difference supplied by its contact with the outside. An animal's memory is merely the sense of its own needs and
of the environment to which its needs are adapted. It
recognizes and remembers as it knows, that is, it has a
knowledge limited to the objects capable of exerting an
action on its activity.

The need is a kind of negative image of the satisfaction it calls forth; it is the subject's constant representation of the object which is meant to fulfill it. This need
is constant, so is the energy which urges the living being
to seek outside itself that which will satisfy it; the qualities of the external object are arranged to concur in this
end, and, so are the identifying signs, owing to which
this object can be *recognized*, (for nothing is known, if
not known in advance). The animal which needs a
fruit or a tree on which to climb will (even when helped
by no experience) keep the tree and the fruit in his
memory, together with the action their presence makes
possible. The same need will arouse the same tension,
which had resulted in the obtaining of the object capable of satisfying it. But man is in a state of need, of
sensitivity in connection with all objects surrounding
him, among which none is *indifferent* to him. Since he
is able to guide his intention, since, by virtue of his attention, he gives to the use of his senses the duration
necessary for the abstraction of the elements he seeks,
since he is able to produce and to continue the effort

which results in the perception of the thing in its effective power and in the latter's signs, he is also capable of repeating this effort. Experience circumscribes man and acquaints him with all the points with which he was meant to be simultaneously born and connected.

This knowledge is an abstraction: it means that we perceive, in the object, different qualities to which we successively apply our attention, served by one or more of our sense devices. We notice that these qualities form groups, that is, that a certain sensation will always be accompanied by certain others, simultaneously, or in a given order. This sensation becomes a sign, a notification of representation. A combination of signs defining an object completely by means of their reciprocal connections, constitutes an *image*. A unique touch is thus sufficient to give us the notion of a certain thing, that is to indicate the state of knowledge we must reach in order to correspond to its state of existence.

We can emphasize the signs which give us an idea about things, like the ones they themselves exhibit, and, in this way, manufacture others at will, and stamp them. For things we cannot constantly have under our eyes, such as, for example, a flower, let us imagine a sign, whose significance in our eyes should depend on us only: "a flower," behold it. If we cannot produce the object, we can, at least, produce within ourselves a state, which is the equivalent of knowledge, which symbolizes it in our eyes, being the sign we consider characteristic of it. To produce, is to endow an artificial, uniform being, leaving always the same imprint on our senses, with a superficial existence. This being is what we call *a word*. I utter and hear it. I receive and give it; I am the instrument and the ear; in its sonority, I perceive myself.

We are right in saying that words are the symbols we use to call things; indeed, we *call* them, we evoke them by creating within us the state of knowledge which corresponds to the feeling of their presence. When I say "the rat" or "the sun," I substitute for the rodent or for the luminous orb, for a given rat, jumping out of the garbage can, for a specific country or city sun, its value, the symbol under which we classify all the impressions with which it can provide us. The word makes me master of the object it represents; I can carry it with me wherever I please, I can act as if it were there.

To name a thing is to repeat it in summary form; it means substituting for the time it takes to be the time we need to pronounce it. The only thing that is left of a thing in this symbol of it, which is a word, is its sense, its intention, all it wants to express as we express it in its place. We adapt this sense to ours, we assimilate it and it becomes the substance of our *intelligence*.

("*Intelligere*," to read in. "To read," to assimilate the sense to our sense. "To comprehend," to perceive at the same time, to combine, by taking in—from obsolete Latin "hendere." Things are taken (comprehended), just as one says that the public is taken with an idea, or that a certain color takes, and that is how we take or comprehend it).

Words can be divided into two categories: one kind serves to designate us, to emphasize the various states of our sensitivity, according to their strength or according to the pleasure or pain we feel; they constitute, to a certain degree, the graduation of our apparatus of knowledge, the play of attitudes, applied to the same agent. The others designate various states of our sensitivity, as produced by the same cause, or this very cause outside ourselves. The first category provides us with ideas on more or less, on compliance or refusal; we dispose of measure and control; something rings according to the tension and the drive. The latter is the inventory of the various objects life proposes to us. Every "proposal" is first of all the enunciation of relationships, of the equilibrium we establish between the thing and us, between subject and object, of the effects on ourselves we are willing to admit, the gesture by means of which we show each other things and show ourselves to them.

But we can do more. The word is not merely the formula of the object. It is the image of myself as informed by this object. When I think "the dog," all I am doing is immediately modulating, disposing the various images and impressions conditioned by this animal. When I say: "the dog barks," it is the dog of my thoughts which barks, the assimilated dog to which I impart my energy as a subject; I summarize the action, I become myself its author, the actor.

It is very important that this, the difference between the terms "knowledge" and "intelligence," to "learn" and to "comprehend," be well understood.

Knowledge is a realization. We run the finger of our sense over the various objects which surround us, we outline, we establish their image, we determine their symbols, we catalogue them, we procure the means to call as well as to recall them, we build up our own vocabulary. Thus, we have within reach a miniature creation, of which we dispose at will, like a child of the animals of his ark. We can manoeuver its parts as we see fit, put them together or disperse them as we like, examine or distribute them; we can imagine any combination convenient to us, arrange scales and bouquets. Since our will is not determined *ad quid,* like that of animals, it does not accept ready made motives for its actions, it must make up its own reasons. Just as it has the faculty of picking the elements of its determination, wherever it wants, so it also has that of incorporating them into an effective and complete image, into the object to reach or the inconvenience to be warded off. The immense task shared by all consists in comparing everything, in trying everything with everything. In practice, we do not cease being tormented by needs. The need concerns things we do not possess, things we are compelled to find on the outside. We "recognize" these things through certain signs; bread, for example, by its smell, that is at the point of contact between their series and ours, and the proposition is the relation we suppose between the sign and the thing it represents. We can apply the value of the sign to anything, according to our fantasy, provided our guide leads us to the object we seek. Once found, the image, in turn, determines our action. In a word, by means of the articulation of its various elements, we must create the figure, the medium according to which we are capable of contacting and knowing.

Knowledge comes from within ourselves, it is the reading at every moment of our position in the whole; intelligence, from the things we know. The first is an estimate of the form; the second, an evaluation of the power. The one evokes the whole by means of a part, the other, mimics, from sense to sensation, the relaxation of the principle into its use, power into action. The one presents a view of the whole, in its defensive structure; the other is an intuition of the element in its general lines of attack. Comprehension is the act by which we substitute ourselves for the thing we comprehend; we take it with us, we take its name, by ringing it like a hammered sound. This name is an incantation formula we use to provoke a certain state of our personal tension, corresponding to a given external object, and which may hereafter serve as its image, starter, *key*. It is a force which acts upon us and which finds in us the means of being recorded and fixed like temperature on a thermometer, like voice on a cylinder. We are now capable of *representing* it by means of the name we give to it. And it expresses to the outside the order it used to be within us, "the word" is thus given to us. This word which we pronounce *call* lends us its sonority to call, to summon (we express the being) the differentials destined to fecundate its natal effort, by representing it. The meaning of expressions such as: to comprehend * a figure, a theorem; to comprehend a line of reasoning; to comprehend a flower, a man; to comprehend music; to comprehend a given type of business, a man's profession, becomes thus obvious. It means to apprehend a principle and its action, to repeat it to the instrument of one's mind, to "think," that is to evaluate the weight and tension of all things. And we are free to use, at will, from now on, the thing represented by the name with which we have provided it, to utilize its services for the satisfaction of our needs, to carry it around as an instrument of comparison and discovery, to challenge with it the unknown surrounding us, in order to deduce an answer and a sign. We disguise ourselves in its likeness. We borrow its creative power, that is the force which creates it. We know what it is and we understand what it does.

* TRANSLATOR'S NOTE: "Comprehend" is used extensively instead of understand, in order to remain in keeping with the explanation given on p. 59 and with the obvious connection between comprehend, apprehend, etc. cherished by the author.

But it is about time to explain the word "We," and passing from the object to the subject, to discuss the knowledge and the intelligence we have about ourselves.

ARTICLE FOUR

ARGUMENT

ARTICLE FOUR.—On Consciousness.—To know oneself. Idea of separation and source included in the word *self*. Source or getting away in comparison with that which is by itself, namely, that which makes things intelligible by establishing the starting and final positions: transcendent God. Inner consciousness of secession. All that which is outside God is in a state of flight or movement. Movement coming from elsewhere is the first feeling of oneself. Secondly, each movement is directed towards the end which fixes or forms it. To know oneself in connection with the outside world is to be produced in relation with one's ends or forms as a whole. To know oneself is to offer oneself as a means of knowing and being connected with the outside world; for the living being, that means to create, as together with himself, all the objects he knows and whose common image he is. He is the starting point of series of movement, departing from all sides. For the animal, to know itself, means to develop the special state of energy, called forth by the motives which surround it and are needed by its own structure. The individual being knows himself first as a force, then as an image, and finally as a cause or "reason." The intelligent being consummates things within himself, he is that which makes them *spirit*, which makes them intelligible by giving them their starting and final positions. Consciousness is the reaction of exerted energy. First traces and evidence of Consciousness: birth, reproduction, the animated being which knows what it has to do. Man possesses, besides his body, a spirit, that is, the psychic movement, in its pure and metaphysical state, a cause, a *reason* conscious of itself. He is its master, that is, he does not feel only its impetus, but also its reaction on himself, reaction to which God's judgment constrains him. Thus, he knows himself first in the autonomous action he exerts on his source, acting as the effect as well as the starter of this cause; he constructs and instructs himself, he molds himself, in contact with the series of causes he sets in motion. Consciousness is the faculty, by virtue of which man knows what he is doing, and, consequently, if his actions are good or bad.

Let us return to the initial verb, whose grammar we are here devising. All verbs express an action, all actions imply an act. We call the verbs active or neutral, depending on whether the act carried out or the thing done has an existence independent of the subject producing it or is merely a state of this subject.[1] So, the neutral co-naître (simultaneously to be born and know) means to produce within myself that without which the rest could not exist for me, and *to* know is the accusative of that without which the subject could not be that which it is. Let us consider now the reflexive form *to know oneself*. We shall first examine the object "oneself," then how it is possessed by the verb.

[1] When abstract nouns do not express adjectival qualities, they are merely verbs made objective by the resection of the subject.

The double term *oneself* has an authentication value; it certifies its identity in all the portions of its duration.

The most essential idea included is that of separation. The motive power is separated from the motionless by movement, and from another motive power by a different movement. And this difference calculates the *power* which is expressed by weight.

Oh, forbearing reader, ferreting out an elusive vestige, the author—who led you up to this point by pushing forward his arguments as Cacus used to push forth the stolen cattle he guided towards his cavern— wishes you to stay in good health. Slippery is the tail of the two-horned cow! Take this ill-treated animal back to its legitimate manger, and reward it for the rich gift of milk and dung! As for myself, I go back with free hands to the pipe and the drum, closing behind me the door of the Lodge of Medicine. Why did I ever promise to give you knowledge of yourselves, when you can get it by merely closing your hand, at the extremity of your arm? But if it be interesting to follow with a magnifying glass perfecting the eye, the intricate design of the initial letter on withered paper, how much more so the orotund word, the active shot of a man flying on his two feet! As he marks the universe with his cross, as he operates his ratchet-wheels and his levers! Here and there, I see a rumpled face starting to bubble, pain or laughter, the clamor of the black circle which is its

mouth spreading all over its scrawling features, like
dimples piercing the surface of boiling water. How he
agitates all his limbs! How he works his pointed hands!
I consider him. I sit down and think.

I have withdrawn my feet from the earth, my hand
from all hands, my senses from all outside objects, my
soul from my senses. I am no longer limited except by
my sense of self, overhearing myself. I am like a wheel
detached from its belt. There is no man left, there is only
one movement left, there is but one movement, there is
but one origin. I suffer birth. I am foreclosed. When I
close my eyes, nothing is left outside me, I am outside.
I am maintained: beyond the place, I occupy a spot. I
cannot go any further; I bear my source.

God being all existence, cannot permit anything else
to exist, except as excluded from Him in its own way.
Man, this vertical witness, analyzes matter and finds
only the purely mathematical fact, movement. Everything perishes. The Universe is but a total way of not
being that which is. So let sceptics talk on, how great is
the security of our knowledge! Indeed, and together
with us, the world exists; of course, it exists, since it is
that which is not.

God alone is that which is: we can add to His ineffable name only the adoration of the essential creative
difference vested in Him, by bearing witness, with the
Angels, to His *Sanctity*.

The primal element of all sciences, the mathematical

root (*math*, to learn) is the structure, the factual realization of our difference. This realization has two modes, the second alone applying to our origin unto God. By virtue of knowledge, we feel ourselves to be complementary; by conscience, we feel our difference; being within the world, we feel outside God.

What I call the feeling of the stem is therefore a human characteristic, the feeling of origin, the religious sentiment (*religare*), the mysterious placentary attachment. And the other aspect of the same idea is that of consciousness, or the feeling of secession. Man is an excluded principle, a foreclosed origin. In relationship to the world, he is entrusted with the part of origin, of *setting up* the principle according to which everything is organized (*setting up*, somehow as it might be said that Ulysses set up for a beggar or Thersites for a prince), he is general, he is the seal of authenticity. With regard to God. He is the delegate to external relations, the *representative* and the plenipotentiary.

Now that we have decided upon the origin and the principle of the complete and self-sufficient being, we may think that nothing exists outside him, except in the state of play and of contradiction. The Being is impassive (I speak roughly, being compelled to use negations to express the very essence of the Act; all that which is, is movement. The Being is one); the thing which is, repeats the unit by multiplying its presence. The Being is infinite, being bound but by Himself; the thing which is, undefined, like the number of positions it is liable to occupy. All created things acquire, because of the fact that they do not come by themselves, a sense, the general transcription of which is movement, flight. They point to their origin, by straying. Movement is not a passive state, it is the first feeling the element has about itself, by not coming *from* itself.

To flee. I must now embed in the course of this discourse a second word: *to resist*. This resistance, this term opposed to flight is designated under the name of *end*, or *finis*. (This is the origin of expressions such as to *define*, *finality*, etc. A thing does not exist, unless it is *finished*.)

Movement in itself, as studied by mathematics, considered purely as the repetition of the unit, is merely an abstraction of the mind. Any movement is limited by an end, which is the production, the birth of a being, something which is capable of *ending*. The body in motion, facing its end from all sides, makes, out of the boundaries it discovers, a closed form or figure. It constructs for its own use, an enclosure it cannot escape. It acquires knowledge of itself in relation to the outside through the various parts united in the common effort which leads them on. And *nature* in its entirety is busy being born. *To be born* (with a negative initial),* that

---

* TRANSLATOR'S NOTE: Here again the author plays on sounds; être (Fr.)—to be; naître (Fr.)—to be born; Claudel considers naître as the negation of être, since except for the *n*, the pronunciation is similar; thus, to be born, negation of to be, as above.

is to be that which is not, that is the image of that which is; the ending and ended image of that which has no beginning. But no thing can be ended except by another thing; no thing can be the complete image by itself, no thing can be, by itself, all that which is not. Everything seeks everywhere its *end*, complement or efference, its part in the composition of the image, the word which expresses its *sense*. And the total word, is *universe* ("universe," version of unity), that which decides upon the sense and the duty. We shall define the first state of conscience in its pure unadulterated form: the sentiment of duty towards the outside, the sentiment of one's duty to the image, the duty of the just toward everything.

The first duty of the material universe, distributed in the form of its components' services, is to endure. God exists: the universe endures, meaning, that it is, at any moment, identical to that which is no more. God exists and the universe resists, that is, it feels itself in all its parts as the thing it cannot be, each of them passing thus through a particular ordeal. God exists and the universe assists, that is it gives itself assistance in its various organs. Nothing can escape. All passes, and since nothing is present, everything has to be *represented*. I put in an appearance. I constitute. I maintain myself in form and figure. I make myself known. I answer the roll-call. The universe, prisoner of its form, provides for the maintenance of the figure, for the necessity of simultaneous birth-knowledge, in compliance with its duty of being known. It constructs its form, its formula and its enclosure, it is incarcerated within its *boundaries,* from which it cannot escape; it cannot cease being present, since it is the constant image of that which is not before that which is.

Each being is born and knows itself as part of the whole towards the maintenance of which its tension or weight strives; the living being starts knowing itself in the form of an image. The physical body preserves that which continues; the living body, capable of beginning and ending, expresses, enunciates, personifies a given moment, the hour. The first appears on the spot to which it owes its existence in duration. The mute mass *summons* God to sow it with a word, to give it that by which it might become capable of coming to an end, and expiring in Him, of returning that which it had received. And, hark, life vibrates in its bosom. Behold, the face vegetates! The living being is the agent and the author of its own movement, of its birth. For it, to know itself, means to make itself known, to offer itself as a means of contact-knowledge, to cause all objects it knows to come to life through and with itself; to become their common symbol, the passing image of the moment when they shall be able to tolerate this tie between them. It is entrusted with the task of summarizing every hour and of consummating that which is not, by consuming it. The image is not a portion of the whole, but its symbol, that which it makes; in the image, as in a coin engraved with the head of the monarch, the whole returns that which it had received.

We arrive thus at the second degree of the knowledge of oneself. The living being must know itself, that is, know the world which surrounds it and conceive it as an image. But this image is not merely the inert molding of the vacuum that irreducible terms leave between them. It is not included, it is adapted. There are no walls around it, but starting points. It is similar to a key whose figure would be the form of its movement adapted to the sluice in which it is inserted. Series of moving bodies expect to be released by it. The living being must fulfil its task. It is responsible and spontaneous. It is not an impulse from the outside, that it must passively transmit. It must work out its act, create that which is required, it must know what it is doing; and, whatever it is doing, it is itself in a state of power or effort. Being an individual, it is interested in each act as a whole; it recognizes itself in each one of them.

Things are not merely objects of knowledge, but also motives of simultaneous birth-knowledge. They call forth, they determine in the subject, all the attitudes implied in its structure. They rouse in it an animated image, their common symbol. They provide it with the means of simultaneous birth-knowledge, of knowing itself in relationship with them, of producing and guiding the force necessary to guarantee the contact between the two terms. In order to achieve this, the object is compelled to appeal to basic resources, to its *nature*, to its essential difference, to the energy which maintains it, that is helps it to produce itself constantly in its present form. To the animal, to know itself means to develop the special state of energy called forth by the *motives* which surround it and which its own structure consigns it, the special movement which animates it and which is responsible for its form, its soul.

Thus the individual knows himself first as a power. We have seen that he knows himself also as an image. And now, he knows himself as source and as reason. His movement is the image, as well as the origin of the phenomena he determines, an operating image, and, in a certain way, already, if I may say so, an intelligent one. It is, indeed that which permits different things not only to know one another but to understand one another. Whereas the living being is the outside cause of its acts, movement is the reason for its form. Form is officially defined as "that which makes a thing what it is." We have seen that a thing is what it is, due to the necessity of corresponding with, of simultaneously contacting and knowing that which it is not, of being, in itself alone, the absence of all the others, of existing in common with that in which they are included. Any living person is an intelligence operating blindly. He is that which brings things back to reality, which liberates them from their appearance, from the enduring image in which they have been held prisoners, the double selective and elective action which enables them to pass, that is, to go elsewhere. Intelligence is that which consumes things, in other words that which reduces them to spirit, that is the movement in which they discover the living being in their flight, and the movement, at its beginning and its end, the proportion and idea of which is reconstructed by the living being within its own body. It is the comprehending and consuming image of things, the intelligible host in which they are consumed.

God constantly secures witnesses of His creation. They have to bear testimony in various ways, according to their order.

The first state of the appearance in court of the simultaneous birth-consciousness of oneself, of the work of the being which takes itself as an object, is that of the vegetable whose life consists in feeding itself, in filling and expanding the form attributed to it, like an empty envelope. The introductory act of procedure is to plead, to appear as plaintiff. The vegetable comes to life: from the air in which it welters, from the earth to which it is attached with shackles which can not be broken. Oh, how green it appears to my eyes! And its second function is being simultaneously born and conscious of itself, namely reproducing itself. Just as pure movement is but the displacement of a body which ceases to occupy one spot in order to move to another, so plants produce a second to take over this same image which grows weaker and weaker.

The plant takes care of the edification of its form, the animal is itself entrusted with the preparation of its own, with the use of the movement which *animates* it. The plant is but an image, the animal is an intention. It does not have a place anymore, but a role. It does not simultaneously come to life and know merely like an ornament or an illustration, but like an actor who interpellates and answers. It has a part to play; it plays its own character. It recognizes the parts to which it corresponds, the little world around it, with which it must live in harmony. Already adapted things provide it with the means of carrying out a given form of the special movement it supplies. The plant is witness to their presence, the animal is the lay-clerk of their intention. It simultaneously comes into the world and knows according to the relationship between them and itself, it recognizes itself in them, by the gesture they force upon it, the action they cause it to carry out. Its knowledge of each of them depends entirely upon its efficiency with regard to everyone of them. It knows itself to be complementary to them. It is defined by its own action: for example, the horse is that which runs and the bird that which flies. It is like the verb which is added to the noun to determine the latter's energy and intention. It knows itself as the verb in which various things are simultaneously born and known to each other. The verb which arouses them beforehand and enables them simultaneously to come into being and know each other and which knows itself by uttering itself.

Now, man: how does he know himself and what does he know within himself? What invitation does he receive from the things around him and what answer do they expect from him?

The characteristic of man is his being endowed with *spirit*. To this word are linked the notions of "souffle" (breath) in the "souffle" (breath) of the most subtle element, of movements independent of any matter submitted to the appreciation of senses that is of movement originating from a pure act of will. The existence and quality of a spirit is thus entirely determined by the wish of the will which produced it, its simultaneous birth-knowledge by the relationship it maintains with its generator. The spirit is simple, since, having no matter, it has no component parts, its movement being but the incessant repetition of the attitude or relationship which has fallen to its lot. In the same way, it is incorruptible, since its disappearance can result only from the cessation of the will which produces it, independently of time measured by the escape of matter. It knows, since it has something to know; matter proves its principle by movement, whereas spirit proves it by consciousness. Both are but ways of being different from God. But one departs, the other is that which can not exist elsewhere; the one creates its place, recreates the image of the Creator; the other, being constant in its bearing, does not have to set it up: it is stationary in its posture, it is the passion of difference. Such is the spirit bestowed upon man, such is the contact it suffers, such is the "souffle" (breath) which gave it birth.

This spirit built itself a body. Just as He took pleasure in the universe as in the plastic image of His expanse and strength, God created the animal as a palpable image, enjoying its existence and the relationship it maintains with the things around it. In man, God created an image of His creative activity, an intelligible image, connected with the very flood-gate of inexhaustible life, enjoying the life it confers, the order it creates around it, its boundless nuptials with the first Cause, whose ring it wears on its finger. To know oneself means to produce oneself in correlation. As matter knows itself by means of its activity and of the image it executes, so does the animal know itself as cause, according to the carrying out of its part and according to the gesture forced upon it by its structure and extorted by its surroundings. So does man know himself according to his mode; he is produced in correlation with God, he knows himself, engendered, in his correlation with the generator. As he knows, so does he know himself. He knows the general, in things that is the generating movement which gives them act and form; he knows himself as generator in the production of his own act and form. By means of the body he has constructed for himself and of the senses he possesses, he is interwoven with the phenomena which surround him, he is tuned on the creative act, the scale and reduction of which he comprises within himself, together with the means of measuring its speed and intensity. All things react on him as on their origin. As he knows himself, so he knows himself as their author and master, by the grace of the Author and the Master who put him in *command*.

Thus man knows himself first through the action he exerts on his source, through the way in which he lives. He knows himself, further, as consequence, effect, means, instrument and starter of his own cause. After constructing himself, he now instructs himself. Since the principle of his life is the proposal of a certain difference within himself, the practical application is but its demonstration. Man has been created to be the witness and the interpreter of a certain performance, to determine its sense within himself. He knows himself thus by his step, the span of his hand, the recourse he finds within himself, the amount of facility or difficulty he experiences in using the instruments he possesses. He exercises himself and the key-board of all organs which connect him with the external commotion; his own body constitutes a kind of document in which he follows the action of the spirit which stirs it. He finds out he has tastes and moods, appetites and revolts, a character, temperament, habits, manners and customs, passions which he fights or encourages, according to the guiding of his will. He takes his place and reaches his equilibrium, he knows what is expected of him, and, mastering his instruments, what he must do, according to circumstances.

Man learns from inside by virtue of habit; similarly, he is molded from the outside by shock. And, as he is produced by contact with his origin, so is he defined by his meeting with his end. Just as we say about someone that he understands something about mechanics or painting, so does he acquire a particular knowledge of objects and starting-points and the more or less intense or frequent pressure to be applied upon his sensitive or driving energy. Thus, these objects become a kind of impression of his form, the symbol of his effort, conditioning its effective or ideal repetition, the condition of his sensitiveness and of his action. He does not lack words to designate his actions any more. Owing to the modifications things cause in his vibratory pulsation, they supply him with a means of measuring it and of being different according to its operations. He knows himself to be a function and creates himself as a motor. Under the influences of the energy he controls, like a metal under the internal hammer, he models and reforges his own person.

Thus, conscience is the faculty by virtue of which man knows what he does, consequently, if he acts well or wrongly. Well or wrong, that is according or in opposition to his future or fundamental, real or imaginary ends, according to his fantasy or his duty. Things do not exist alone, they are related by a mutual obligation. This obligation, purely physical and formal (in the plastic sense) in the brute, is moral in the free man. His conscience tells him if he has contradicted in any way his purpose and his nature.

I have finished what I had to say about our knowledge in this life. I have calculated a contour; I have woven a net of sentences similar to cryptographic grates or lace on the window. We are now to discuss that which we can feel of the knowledge reserved for us in the after-life, which has been guaranteed by infallible promises.

ARTICLE FIVE

ARGUMENT

ARTICLE FIVE.—On Man's Knowledge after Death.— Any movement applied to a being has an end which stops it and gives a form to its testimony. The duration of this testimony in a being is proportional to that of the fact it confirms. But man is the witness of permanence and of the variation of things in relationship with a fixed point. Man bears witness of the permanence of speech. In order to bear testimony to the permanence of things, man must be eternal himself, the word being but a modification of the subject. The perishable organs of man are meant merely to borrow from things the modifications of their own movement, using them for their simultaneous birth-knowledge. The end of man being a permanent state, man is naturally imperishable in the entirety of his nature, that is, in the unity between his soul and his body, and their separation is a violent state. That which can be known by the soul when isolated and without any personal organs: its differences. The difference between it and God. The difference between it and other souls, owing to the special intention it expresses. Our own name. Knowledge of other souls from the point of view of their solidarity with its own duty. The instrument for the knowledge of soul in itself is the information given to its essential vibration. Soul knows its intention in full, consequently, it retains the memory of the past which becomes fully intelligible to it. It knows palpable things, since it does not cease knowing them in their supreme cause. Eternal formation.

When a man dies, he ceases to be in relationship to us and, consequently we say that he is no more. Indeed, from that moment on neither our senses nor our spirit discover anything corresponding to the perception whose cause he used to be: he is no more; that is all we know; for us, he is as if he were no more. He does not stand on his feet anymore. He does not produce anymore the energy due to which he was with us. This gone, nothing remains but an inert imitation, a statue of flesh soon to glide away: away with these remains! No matter what the lessons imparted by reason and faith, the beast in us cannot understand anything else:

he was and he is no more, and, to the extent to which we remember him, he is from that moment on, that which is no more.

(Indeed, before his death, man was that which was not; he is, after death, that which is no more: he is no more that which was not.)

"To be born." "To know." How can man continue to be born (naître) once he is dead? And simultaneously with what could he be born and know? Stripped of his senses, what and how could he know?

We have seen that matter is not the cause of movement, but that, on the contrary, movement is the cause of the various combinations to which we give the common name of matter. There is no well defined rough material and, in movement alone, does it find its unity. On the other hand, if matter should have an existence independent of that of the movement which produces, expresses and evaluates it, this is not the place to examine the question. We have seen that our existence and our knowledge, our spirit, our conscience and our senses are equally unable to enunciate or understand anything in us except movement, that is variation as compared with a stationary given point. All the notions about the outside world offered by our organs amount to the variations taking place on the scale of our nervous vibrations. We have further stated that movement owes its form to its *end*, which circumscribes it by putting an end to it. As in the case of the calculated gestures of the sculptor or the surgeon, the impulse which controls its intensity is regulated according to the requirements of the work to be executed. It ceases when its aim or term is reached, that is, when the reciprocal connection brought about by necessity between subject and object ceases. Movement in itself is not extinguishable, its momentary "time" and the rhythm it uses for its special assignment alone come to an end. Supposing that the connection established by necessity between subject and object were permament, the corresponding movement would be permanent as well.

Knowledge implies birth, every substance implies its proof, the multiform verb which tells it what it is in regard to time. The living are a finding-out apparatus: they do not suffer their contour; they must find and establish it themselves. They store, repeatedly, the rough energy they must draw, according to the size of their body, just as the pint is a capacity measure. They transmit it according to the special rhythm of the almost musical idea, the beating of which is included in them and elaborated according to the need of the various organs and the ends for which they are created.

Just as the end in a painting is considered to be that which constitutes the form by limiting the space it occupies, so, in an absolute sense, the end is that which constitutes the form, by furnishing the means and the materials required by its research on the living, so that it might remain such as it is. To find the end means to find the origin. Just as the weevil lives on the lily and the beetle in dung, the existence of the animal is closely linked with that of certain beings which determine it. The duration of its testimony is proportional with that of the fact it confirms.

But the presence of man does not necessarily depend on that of such or such other figures around him, of such or such other situations in time. He is at home everywhere. He knows the "general." In all his forms, he is directed towards the common element which engenders him by means of the specific modification. The animal is constructed, like a toy for a well determined jump. To talk about the knowledge of the monkey, or the bird, or the fish, is to state the modifications that a given interposed object exerts on the tree-climber, the fruit-nibbler, and the under-water swimmer. In his quest for knowledge, he uses the same intention which brought his organs together. Man knows the permanent, meaning that, in each thing, he recognizes variation, as compared with a fixed point, just as the Chinese express the idea of eternity by the character meaning "water," with a dot above. How would he be able to know things, and how could they, in their permanence, have simultaneous births with and knowledge of him, if he were not permanent himself, in his initial breath and in the movement it imparts to his body? Such is the testimony of his permanence that nature asks of God and that man is destined to bring.

The act by means of which man certifies the permanence of things; by means of which, he formulates the
combination of permanent conditions, which, together,
give every thing the right of coming into the spirit's
focus, independently of second circumstances and
causes; by means of which he conceives it in his heart
and repeats the order which created it, is called speech.
To point out the word, we use three terms: verb, word,
noun. The verb expresses the faculty of the speaker;
the word, the special movement which is every being's
motive, illustrated by the speaker's emotions; the noun,[1]
the noun finally (or the *no*), the difference owing to
which no individual is equivalent to another individual.
To name a thing, means to produce it inextinguishable,
for it is to produce it in relationship to its principle
which does not include cessation. I consider a being; I

[1] Every word is the expression of a psychological state, caused by
attention to an outside object. It is a gesture which can be separated
into its component elements or letters. The letter or, more precisely,
the *consonant* is a sonorous attitude caused by the generating idea it
mimics, the emotion, the word. As S, for instance, emphasizes the
idea of scission; N, rendered by the occlusion of the voice, while the
tip of the tongue rising to the palate, suggests the idea of an inner
level reached, of a confession of deafness, of refusal in a latent plenti-
tude. *In, non, hominem, nomen, numen, omnis, nemo, semen, unus,
numerus, nos, nous* (Gr.), and the immense group *noscere, nasci*; the
form of the present participles (Fr. ending *ant*).

"Cratylus is right in his statement that there are natural names for
things, and that not all men are artisans of names, but only those who
consider each name from the point of view of its natural fitness to
each thing, and its ability to reproduce the idea by means of its letters
and syllables."

PLATO, *Cratylus.*

seek the pure existence in it, the special movement which breeds it, and whose mathematical formula does not include its dissolution in itself (nor any other beginning than the advent before the spirit), and tolerates the ending of its operation only by an intervention from the outside, and for the good of a wider order. Movement is a self-repetition (or birth) which takes place more or less frequently in relationship with an immutable principle. In order to exert knowledge, that is, in order to reproduce each one of the special movements in its state of correlation with the origin; in order to determine within me the internal state corresponding to each of them, in a word, in order not to be compelled to a limited number of rhythms, on the contrary, in order to have the means to supply an image for each one, I must possess the faculty of *setting* myself according to their common principle, I must be in contact with it, or, be permanently different from it, which is the same thing. In order to consolidate things in their quality of terms, by calling them *inexterminable*, I must be inexterminable myself. The word does not imply death; the word is one of my states.

And yet, we notice that man's organs are not fundamentally different from those of the perishable animal. Their activity is fed and distributed by apparently similar processes. We live, we die in the same way. What movement then should survive in the body it animates, like rotation, for example, in the wheel?—I answer that movement is not, in itself, extinguishable, but merely the combination of special movements we know as bodies. Indeed, each movement being but the reproduction of a certain existence, can always be added to itself like 1 to any given sum, and is not submitted, to any limitation of duration by nature. What this existence is, fundamentally, we do not know, for, in order to know what it is, we would have to know first that which it is not, that is God; its essential trembling before the face of the Holy One. The existence of a movement is limited only by its end, by the purpose of nature and by the purpose of God; in the animal, by its palpable knowledge and, in man, by his intelligible knowledge, which is everlasting like God Himself, under the palpable images which form his object. It is only natural that man, in need of knowing material things, should draw them from his surroundings, like the animals, from the movement necessary to his simultaneous birth-knowledge, but he digests and converts this movement, he instills it with commotion, with the intention which is his own; he connects it with the continuous source of his own being, contained within him: his gesture is but the translation of the original sob, in terms of the material universe. That to which this new rhythm is imparted is eternal like its end, no matter whether his organs of amplification, constructed and maintained by him, subsist or not.

One should not think that the spirit of man is joined

to his body like steam to the machine when it is introduced into the slide-valve, or the content to its container,
or that any one organ acts as its support. What place
could it occupy, since it has no parts? The essential
movement of the animal is that unto which it constructs
its body, through which it simultaneously comes into the
world and knows. The action of this movement may be
permanent or momentary, according to the nature of
the ends towards which it strives. We have seen that
man's is permanent, namely, it leads him to know God
in His creatures. "God's will is without compunction."
Man is therefore permanent, like the end to which he is
dedicated. Incorruptible in his soul as in his body, the
soul's necessary instrument, man's death is a violent
accident. The removal of the end's intention, the with-
holding of its means of achieving this end, and of obtaining the materials necessary to its maintenance constitutes
a disorder which should be viewed as the effect of the
primitive transgression. When man was created, he
had an equal knowledge of his beginning and his end.
Seduced by the serpent, he indulged in the idea of his
end, as though it had been the product of his own
mind and not of the will of God, Whose instrument he
was. This is why an end was finally given to him in the
death of his body, which enabled him to reach it. He
became aware only of his end and his origin in the
Father was concealed from his eyes; flesh constitutes a

wall between us and God.[1] Then comes death, reversing
the terms, and delivering him, despoiled and defenseless,
to the Judgment of Eternity and of the source which
created him. He can no longer hide his nakedness
under the leaves like Adam. He looks and can find no
end around him. He has taken possession of the entire
part of creation in the center of which he had been
placed, he has used and abused it as though it were his
personal property, and now he must answer for it to
the legitimate owner. Behold, he stands stripped, he
stands naked before the stern Eyes. Behold, he ap-
proaches God for judgment, in his nakedness, in the
simplicity of his intelligent will, in the direct contempla-
tion of his duty. Frightening obligation, when lacking
the grace granted freely, which alone could fulfill it!
Oh, to be able to sustain, for my purification, for my
glory or for my torture, the eyes of the Almighty Who
is all life. Later, as the souls survive for the Day of
Judgment, their respective bodies will be reunited with
them, and man will be consolidated again, body and
soul, unto Judgment. But I propose to discuss only the
knowledge of separated souls. And since God became
their object, we must find out their knowledge in God
and God's knowledge in them.

This is to know, as I have repeatedly shown, their essential difference. But what difference between the now

[1] En ipse stat post parietem.—Cant. II. 2.

separated spirit and God, and between the simple and the simple, when, according to the Philosopher, any difference is comparable to the addition of a number or to the subtraction of the unit? Neither the soul, nor God has parts; and thus, the differences existing between them can not be conditioned by the presence or absence of one of them. I believe that they differ first of all by nature, since God exists through Himself and the soul through God. God is the substance; the soul is the image, but an image of God in His entirety, since its object is not divided. The rest of creation is not, properly speaking, an image, but a symbol, as color is the symbol of light, incessantly striving to constitute itself, in order to be able to scatter. Secondly, the question of finiteness does not differentiate the soul from God alone, but also from other souls, each being endowed with a special mode of finiteness. Heat is different from electricity and the latter from light by the number of vibrations producing them; one metal from another, by its specific weight; spiritual species are different from one another, one angel from another, owing to the indissoluble figure which formulates them; while, within the species, all human souls vary by the use in view of which they have been given life. A human soul is the effect of a special will, not the image of partial entity. It varies according to the underlying intention, not the substance. Intention is the attention to the end. The intention of the soul, the attention of God directed toward the end to which it is destined. The orders of Angels vary according to the functions they are to perform; similarly, men vary because they are dedicated to the knowledge of bodily things and each man, in turn, is unlike the others depending on the nature and the degree of simultaneous birth-knowledge he is destined to acquire, depending on the portion and the moment of creation whose oblat and witness he is forever called upon to be in God's eyes.

This is therefore the "new name" mentioned by the Gospel, this proper name by virtue of which we have been called upon to come to life for eternity, this ineffable name destined to remain forever a secret between the Creator and ourselves, and entrusted to no one else. To learn this name means to understand. To learn this name means to understand our nature, to feed ourselves with our reason for existing. Just as words are made out of vowels and consonants, our soul, with each breath, draws, from God, sonority in all its plenitude. To come to life would thus be, for our soul, to know, to be fully conscious. *Tunc cognoscam*, says the apostle, *sicut et cognitus sum*. We shall then see the number expressing unity, the essential rhythm of this movement which constitutes my soul, this measure which is myself. We shall not only see it, we shall be it, we shall produce ourselves in the perfection of freedom and vision and in the purity of perfect love. We shall draw from the Lamb's bosom our means of being different from Him so that we might have something to offer to Him. In the bitterness of mortal life, the most poignant ecstasy revealed to our nature is the one accompanying the creation of a soul, through the coupling of two bodies. Alas, it is but the humiliated image of the substantial embrace, in which, learning its name and the intention it satisfies, the soul shall utter and make itself known; it shall, in succession, aspire and expire itself. Oh, continuation of our heart! oh, incommunicable word! oh, action in the future Paradise! All carnal possession is incomplete in its span and its duration and how despicable its rapture, compared with the undescribable beatitude of those nuptials! Oh, God, Thou feedest us with the bread of tears; and givest us tears to drink in great measure.[1] Is any conquest of an empire, any possession of a woman's body comparable to God's laying hold of us by our soul, as lime takes hold of sand, and what death (death our very precious patrimony) enables us to offer, at last, such a perfect holocaust, such a generous restitution, such a filial and tender gift? This is the reward promised to all the righteous and the unique salary which fills the workers of the parable with surprise. But, in reality the dowry of each soul shall be different from the other, like the will whose expression it is, like the intention which endowed it with life.

And, by an exquisite inversion, the things I say to you explain the suffering of the damned.

[1] Ps. LXXX, 5.

The soul alone shall know God; the dogma of the Communion of Saints teaches us that it shall also know the other holy souls which enjoy the same vision.

This knowledge may be obtained and exerted in two ways.

The soul separated from the body knows God, it knows Him entirely, since this object of its knowledge is one and does not have any parts; but this knowledge is the soul's own, that is, able to give it the life of the image or *person* it is. As it comes to realize fully the intention it carries out, it shall notice that this intention is special, that is, that it is connected to a more general intention. The soul feels, inside itself, this total energy, the initial commotion, not of God, who is an invariable act, but of the mystic difference which gives birth simultaneously to all creatures linked together by the blessed vision. It understands that, alone, it cannot exhaust all the gratitude and that it needs the help of all the other spirits. Just as it recognizes, in the special act of love which is responsible for its creation, the very necessity implying the creation of the other complementary spirits, so it needs their voices, in order to join its own to theirs. It sees in itself, and in its roots in God, those of all the other souls linked together by a common love. It needs all of them, all play a part in the economy of its Salvation, from the Virgin and the Highest Angel, to the smallest infant the midwife has hardly had time to baptize.

Not only do the souls know one another in God, they also possess a direct means of knowledge. Just as bodies perceive bodies and matter apprehends matter, so do spirits discern spirits.[1] We have seen that the apparatus of sensible knowledge consists of vibration, that is, of a certain regulation of the intimate rhythm on which are inserted the external impressions. We have defined each *measure* of the vibration as a recurrence of birth. But birth does not apply only to bodies, but also to spirits. Thus, the spirit being capable of vibrating, is also capable, in the outline drawn by its intervals, of receiving the impression of other homogeneous substances. There is a spiritual expanse where "distances" are set by harmonic relations, instead of tactile displacements. Souls shall no longer exert knowledge of one another by signs any more, but by their very birth.

Now, we have to find out what knowledge of material things and of the spirits not yet separated can be had by the spirits separated from their bodies. Man, like all created things, being endowed with movement, acquires, by this very fact, a direction, a sense, an intention and an end. Possessing a spirit, he is conscious of

[1] Et quoniam ipsa eorum claritas vicissim sibi in alternis cordibus patet, cum uniuscujusque vultus attenditur et conscientia penetratur. Ibi quippe uniuscujusque mentem ab alterius oculis membrorum corpulentia non abscondet, sed patebit animus . . . atque unusquisque tunc erit conspicabilis alieno, sicut nunc esse non potest conspicabilis sibi. . . . Unde dicitur: Nolite judicare ante tempus, donec veniat Dominus qui et illuminabit abscondita tenebrarum, et manifestabit consilia cordium (I Cor., IV, 5). Auro clara, vitro perspicua—S. Greg. *De auro et vitro.*)

this intention, but, separated from God during his life-
time, he is informed by the outside only, by the term
which stops him, by the various parts of the outside
world with which he comes in contact. Separated from
his body, he acquires, in God alone, the steady point
which determines his *sense and direction*, independently of the perceptible guiding marks or bearings.
In seeing God fully, he realizes perfectly, by the very
fact of his nature, his constitutive difference or intention. Man's intention, his power (as one says the power
of a machine) is directed towards action on external
things; this action results in a sensation and a movement, an elicited image of itself. For the creature moves
away from vision only in order to work at this image.
Deprived of its senses, the soul separated from the body
does not possess the means of receiving outside information; but it is not bereft of the initial sense, constituted
by its shifting connection with the only fixed point.
Now, the soul takes up directly the thrust and the
design of the impulse which, not long ago, used to set
going the various apparatus of the senses, supplying it,
in this way, with the perception of its image. In the
"time" allotted to its tension, it folds up in all its might;
it no longer possesses the means of creating images
with its senses; but the organization owing to which
it used to set them going constitutes a kind of image
in itself. It builds itself up in a certain state of equilibrium; it founds, alone, without any help, the in-

telligible figure, for the creation of which it used, here-tofore, the external circumstances. This image consti-tutes the soul's gift to its Creator, achieved by the second measure of its respiration, and the substance of its joy or its torment. The now fully understandable aspira-tion, the intake it carries out by itself in God, and by means of which it expands and spreads out before His eyes in all the powers of nature, replaces the blind afflux used heretofore for its good or bad actions; its *motives* are taken up again and checked in their detail, by the living light; I say approved or reproved, depending on whether or not they comply with the image predeter-mined in us by God.

This is the knowledge of its past that the soul takes with it into death; but what about that which it might exert, from beyond the grave, over palpable things?

According to our definition, in a broader sense, to know, is also to exist. Thus, all that which is born, spirit or body, exists and knows at the same time, according to its own world. There is harmony in each breath of dura-tion, in all the parts of creation, from the Seraph to the worm. Thus, since the soul does not cease being born, it does not cease to exist and know. It is part of an equi-librium and of a whole, the variations of which it feels deep within itself. Since the separated soul is pure intelligence, all birth from it is the substance of clear knowledge, and, consequently, of all concerted causes which affect it. Whereas, in this life, intelligence is informed by the senses, in the next, the very substance of the intelligible soul shall constitute its perceptive organ, in obtaining the arrangement, the proper balance of forces corresponding to a given sensitive state. Evidently, the soul is more actively interested in those parts of the whole with which it finds itself most directly connected, that is, in a relationship of causation or proximity, according to the figures of spiritual distances, determined above. It suffers all the consequences determined by its good or bad actions.

The simplicity as well as the immense variety of the state of knowledge which will be the soul's, once it is separated from the body after death, becomes thus apparent. The essential organ of this knowledge will be the double measure of consciousness, expressed, during this life, by breathing, heart-beats, the sharp and the flat, the short and the long syllables, the fundamental iambus of all language. But, whereas, our existence down here is like a barbaric and broken language, our life in God shall be like exquisitely perfect verse. Indeed, as we have seen, the word is not merely the symbol of a certain state of our sensitivity, it is the evaluation of the effort we have to make in order to produce it, or rather to produce ourselves in it. The poet, master of all words, the poet, whose art it is to use them, is expert in stirring us to a state of harmonious and intense, precise and strong intelligence, by a clever disposition of the objects they represent. But, in the after-world, we shall be the *poets,* the makers of ourselves. This keen sense of our essential prosody, this impossibility of escaping our admirable measure shall then be conferred to us directly, without the empirical and hazardous intervention of external language.

But the incantation down here is not strong enough to preserve the elements of our body which are required for other needs. However, in spite of everything, even in this perishable world, eternity, in its circulatory form, presents no unfamiliar or difficult problem to a mind clinging to combinations which are the true object of knowledge; nothing can be defined in terms of beginning or end. We see around us fixed frames, filled with matter in movement. The idea of eternity amounts to that of an *enclosure* infrangible in itself. All *forms* are deduced from this same idea of an enclosure *closed* on itself, and we have seen that, in this world, nothing can exist without a form. Then, Time shall be closed on us, and the Present shall be its eternal center. The time once established, hark, the choir bursts out singing! What can be better done than that which is accomplished? What can be more finished than that which is ended? What can be more ended than that which cannot be ended any more? Then, our knowledge shall be complete, like our form and like our enclosure. Just as the day, never the same, repeats the day, and the year repeats the year, just as the screw of stars tightens or loosens, at regular intervals, and just as the children of Night widen or narrow the reel, like the motion of lips, without ever breaking it (so are these nations of ether scattered or sluiced, like a crowd which cracks and moves, driven by the same heart), so shall our occupation, in eternity, consist in the accomplishment of our part toward the perpetration of the Office, the maintaining of our equilibrium, always new in the immense contact with all our brothers, the raising of our voice in the unvoiceable lamentation of Love!

The Development of the Church

THE DEVELOPMENT OF THE CHURCH

FROM THE DEPTH of the sacred woods, from the height of the full-grown primitive forests, whose shadow still conceals the sacred huts of Nikko, in Japan, the clearing of ground has, little by little, thinned the veil until it has become no thicker than this single row, this orderly colonnade, enclosing the walled sanctuary of classical temples. For, ever since Paradise, and like Jonah, the day of the repentance of Nineveh, the great city, and Elias, in his sorrow, man has always turned to the tree, shoot and vegetation of the unity, expression of waiting in testimony, seeking it as guardian of his prayers and as protector of his waters; sitting, kneeling in the shadow. But, while the heathen, incapable of subduing mystery, sought its obreptitious darkness as a hiding-place for his dolls, the Christian Church absorbed the mystic forest, adapting its avenues and its choir, from within, for the use of the human congregation.

The pagan temple was, in reality, but the prison and the container of God; because of the case in which it was kept, the tribe asserted its right of ownership over the idol. The box in which the wandering band had carried for so long its now enlarged share of the traditional treasure, *superstition,* consolidated on a permanent foundation, that it seemed of the utmost importance that it should not be found empty. By its silence, concealing the lack of words, certain statues symbolized occupation, common object of antiquity, and faith and worship consisted in a mere excitation of the amulet. That is how, even today, the Mohammedan prays in front of the empty recess from which, he believes, his God retired. But, the act of worship remained mostly outside the temple; under the colonnades, in the exedra and the yards, the processions and the theory continued their search and exodus, until the day of revelation, formulating a legal tie between the Creator and man, established a religious function, in its real and strict form, with the church as its official organ, the common house of God and the initiated man.

That is why the new structure did not borrow any of the principles of its development from the pagan "container." No more mystery room, with oracular powers, the entering of which without preliminary purification, was considered a profanation; all relations, even when God Himself was involved, were resolved by transactions, and in this way the Sacrament now replacing mystery, the church became the transformation of the *market.* The roof is meant simply to furnish shelter. The crossroad, the public street is closed, walled in, like that dark road to Emmaus, where the disciples "constrained" the Saviour to abide "for it was toward evening, and the day was far spent." Inside, at each step, the symmetric spacing of the columns seems to offer the example of the balance which presided at their planting. They lead, they are the rows of witnesses and their choir. Dark promenade hall, avenues of silence, favorable ambushes of grace.

So, the Cathedrals of our old towns are never completely detached from the houses, between which they are more or less caught. Today, a chapel is made especially for the hospital or convent for which it is meant; likewise, in times of old, the greatest vessel inflated by human breath, the church, sprang up from the town and the town arose from the church, closely hugging its flanks, almost under the arms of the Eve of stone. So many thoughts befall the traveller during those wine-colored dusks of France, when, for a moment, before being driven away in his eternal wandering he sees, at the winding of a slow and lazy river, or over there, on the top of some urban mounds, the old black monster, the Evangelic Beast, captured, tied up among the souls, in which it is rooted by its buttresses, enormous chains of stone!

Thus, the aim of the architects of the Middle Ages was not to draw, in mid-air, a temple with the settled and precise lines of a statue, but to close up the mystical market-place, to create shadow forever. All the elements of the building, its vegetation, conspired, for centuries, towards the royal elevation of the baldachin above the hollow cross of the crossroads, symbolizing the meeting with the town, abstract image and seal of the town in its midst. A canopy with low-hanging and ill-joined veils; at each slit of the vessel, doors similar to the distance between two curtains, and the pinion, an enlargement of the doors, of the towers, finally, whose function was to produce, through the open outside spaces, the thunder of the forest entombed with Christ: such are the principles of the Cathedral.

We have decided that the heathen chest was adjusted, like a coffin for the dead, to accommodate the fetish, the enigmatical token bequeathed by the forefathers, the mystery which had to be kept away from open air. But when the Father decided to send his Son among us, the Word Jesus, a speaking man, the earlier echo, confusedly concealed like the sea in the spire of a winding shell, expired in the oracular vase, and between our Saviour and ourselves began this familiar and precise conversation which has never come to an end. Christ was a public man, and, from the very beginning, he made his abode in public places. If we seek Him during the days of His stay among us, we find him in Simon's house and the hostelry of Emmaus and the well of Sychar and always, according to the Pharisees' reproach, with those who "eat and drink"; so also the Church. When it came to life, it was satisfied with the trivial shelter of the basilica, and prepared its ban-

quet there, erect at the crossroads, like the Wisdom of
the Proverbs and like the messengers of the Parable of
Marriage! The profane basilica existed mainly as a roof,
offering a temporary lodging and the shade of a fictitious
garden to passers-by who came to exchange words and
money among themselves. It was merely a gallery made
to be crossed and nothing was there to stop the foot
awhile between the two parallel plans of ceiling and
floor. But from the day when the Church substituted
the permanent altar for the hawker counter, and when
the sacramental transaction replaced the bank and the
market and the scales of commerce and of justice, the
building was truly consecrated to the permanent function, which had come to take place within it; and we see
it, like a man, wrapped up in meditation, create its own
countenance. Until then, the roof had been nothing else
but the severance from the native soil, the raising up of
the sepulchral standard—maintained in the homogeneous
inertia of its weight and its rigidity—by means of walls
and pillars. As soon as the censer starts smoking under
the vulgar hangar, we see the whole structure setting to
work and expanding fully. Roofing is the exclusive in-
vention of man in his desire to complete the enclosure of
this cavity, similar to a tomb or the maternal womb, he
reinstates for the needs of sleeping and eating. Now,
this cavity is entirely filled, swelled as with something
alive. The abode disturbed in the parallel actions of its
weight seeks its common center and finds its equilib-

rium in its own vacuum; the cupola appears, the egg from which each church—up to our days—bursts forth. Gothic architecture is the special development the Middle-Ages drew out of the established principle. But other developments are possible and it seems that a certain law presides over all that has been accomplished in this field since the sixteenth century, in a unity exhibited for the first time, in our days, in the Sacré Coeur.

Thus, the Church, endowed with this principle of expansion, was originally but a collection of tents assembled in one and the same enclosure, of the three tabernacles proposed by Saint Peter, in his vision on Mount Tabor: one for our Lord, the second for Moses and the third for Elias. It was merely the shelter secured in the eucharistic camp, the Caravansary of Abraham and Melchizedek. The three naves were blended into one hall, in a plan, a late example of which is offered by the Cathedral of Poitiers, in spite of the presence of the ogive. But soon, the idea of direction and of an introversive movement was added to that of shelter. For, the Cross, which, according to the sacred promise, was to "draw everything to itself," was planted in the back of the building, in that gesture of widespread arms, pointing, unfolding, calling and stopping; stopping and allowing no one to move further. Thus, one of the two exits of the passage being shut, the crowd, following the central axis, coagulated into a common vision, spread peripherically. Alone, around the altar and the choir, the officiating priests are given their own places; by its very pause, the crowd expresses, by congealment, the movement which has attracted it, a movement determined by a precise act; its partaking of the perpetration of the liturgical drama, in which it communicates for the perfection of the Hour. The middle bay, barred by unfathomable mysteries, guides the eyes up to that point, the aisles lead the step back and forth in their circuit.

This is the reason for the differentiation of the three naves, of the ogive.

In Angoulême, in Périgueux, the succession of cupolas lends to the altar the frame of their range of porches. Then, the juxtaposition of these similar elements had to combine into the unity of the vault and the passage and thus the time came for the temple, in its full evolution, to invent the ogive. The constructive matter had come to life; now, we behold it in full transformation while the church becomes conscious of itself and of its unity. The cupola fitted like a lid, the semicircle of the arch becomes more concave, under the burden pressing upon it; the ogive is the effort to open, the release of the intimate spring. Up to that point, the structure owed its form to the outside, repressed in its expansion, under the weight of piled up stones, solidified in its compact shell. Now that the principle of its development breaks forth from the inside, we witness, by virtue of a natural law, the new power receiving its expression from the vegetative impulse. The precise effort needed explicit terms. In the homogeneous mass of the dome appear the four vigorous nerves which raise and distend it, and all these unfurled branches have their roots in the thick-set stem of the dark Roman forest, which, fashioned by the sap of the future branches, engendered in the shadow, a mustiness of monsters and embryos, covering itself, at the jointure of its capitals, with the pale flora of caves.

When the ogive appears, the idea of enclosure disappears, swallowed by that of absorption, the end of which is the Altar. Instead of the heavy ceilings of the strict passage, with its successive openings, multiplying the thresholds of the penitential prisons and the weight adapted to his kneeling, the worshipper's path toward God, is now open, like a road. With a stroke of its double lever, the ogive, like the humeral effort of two opening wings, forcefully removes the weight of stones heretofore separated from the ground with so much hardship, by so many props, and frees it from sight, by suspending it, through exaltation. Inertia is resolved into opacity and the roof into an overflow of shadow. So that a greater expanse of night may feed the gold of the candles, which, above the altar, proclaim the pure holocaust in the august cavern, protected from the day measured in hours, before the eyes of the living Church assembled! Now, the eyes are no longer shut off brutally beyond the Sacrificer and reverberated by a sort of

Domical vault, as it was in the first churches; the prison has been opened and the stained glass calls the eyes, which allow the mind to tarry on the harmonious forms and the display of colors and to rest in the bosom of light. Light penetrates, splits in innumerable sparkles of silkiness, as if upset by the steady exhalation of incense, like truth through the divisions of the syllogism, including obscurity, like the sun seen through leaves or through the smoke rising from an encampment, in the woods; the priest officiates before the outside opulence of the excluded and gaping world. The soul of the church which used to be diffuse, is now concentrated in the median nave, which, in the double procession leading to the glowing cradle of the apse, with its colossal shafts, allows but a belt of subdued shadow at every step, wavering for a minute from the formidable rectilinear attraction; and, while the ogives, like a forest of branches with their root in the sky, draw towards and tie to it the entire inner framework in a unanimous summit, on each side, the buttresses, like arms harnessed from the outside to the mass, hang on and fasten everything tightly to it, concentrating on the elevation of the Mother-nave and of the main vessel.

The façade being an exhibition, the church, collected on its inner principle, profoundly entangled in the human stuff, can display but its doors.

One can study, in front of the good old church Notre-Dame-la-Grande, in Poitiers, like a leaf in its bud, the shrivelled germ of that which was to become the ample Gothic portal and the complete theme of the gigantic design. The portal is the illustrated title of the book, the external rood-screen, the shifting iconostasis. The lectern, which, in full pomp, the deacon used to mount, preaching the Gospel and proclaiming Easter, was converted into two towers, shaking noisily their convoking bells in the wind. Rank upon rank, angels and kings, patriarchs and pontiffs, the evangelical pageant displays its testimony, in orderly lines, above the triple entrance; they themselves form the door, their bodies tightly squeezed against each other, constituting the transition from that which is on the outside to that which is inside. The aperture is no longer a mere arbitrary ablation of a fragment of the wall, but, yielding to the inner aspiration, it retracts in the animated way of a mouth, and the honorary iris of the saints, kept alive by the wand interspersed with symbols and angels, as a stalk, surrounds, with its palm the nucleus of gaping darkness. Like a notched fruit, the wall calls forth, wherever the iron attacks it, the seeds of life embedded in its texture. The austere primitive church had erected, in front of its doors, the shelter of the narthex for the catechumens and the raving, to whom it forbade its door; today, it delegates the entire stone clergy outside its very doors, to invite the pure and the impure alike, and it opens its ranks to receive them and to let them pass.

And now, church of God, what foliation and what
bushes, what subtle tendrils, the smoke of what pinnacles, what arrows vibrating like the stem of a hyacinth,
will provide you with the innumerable and strange
means of becoming linked with azure and with the
cloud and of hanging the supreme cross to the highest,
if you should not blend with their perfume and their
honey? Neither soft lead nor the best thinned wood can
achieve it; but, I remember one Easter Noon, at Rheims,
when I emerged, like a man bursting forth through the
trap-door into the thundering dove-cot, into the sun and
above the round and gray plain and the lilac-colored
town and in the midst of this nestful of bells, which, in
harmony with the hymn celebrating the canonic Hour,
seemed to put an end to everything in the sky, with a
Hallelujah! The cathedral ends in the wind. Whoever
wants to understand the churches of Rouen, for example, in the middle of the works which flank them, must
remember the villages of Normandy on the slopes north
of the Seine; each of them maintains, for protection, its
squares of beech trees, in which the squalls, coming
from the sea, frolic and then calm down. Likewise, at
Rouen, God's Tree (l'Arbre-Dieu), the Banner of Faith
(l'Etandard de la Foi), churches the obstinate and foolish north wind cannot tear away, look like a tortured
flame, like a buoy tormented by storm, like a giant vegetable being assaulted by an implacable foe and restrain-
ing him with its intermingled limbs. Saint Quen, Saint

Maclou, and I would call even the cathedral itself a fortress of chandeliers, from the center of which bursts forth, at the very intersection of the cross, planted emphatically on the great heavily carved tower, the Arrow, like the Easter Candle, the taper on its candlestick, while the hollowed blocks on each side of the North and South porches suggest enormous lanterns and the bushels of the Parable!

Thus, the consideration of each of the levels of the Cathedral, its pillars, its vaults, its pinnacle, can unveil the characteristics of each of the periods which partook in its development, by the progressive elevation of the generating principle. Toward the end of the Middle Ages, the effort of the ogive had completely exhausted its energy. Under its tension, the pillars had unravelled into a cluster of little columns, the partition-walls, open on all sides, had transformed the dark vessel, powerfully fortified with enormous muscles, into a glass-cage, encompassed by a slender armor of buttresses and frame-works, a fervent gem with an inner fire, oriented, with pious art, toward the sun-beam, to digest and distil its gold. These too slender pinnacles seem to call for the axe! and the eye still suspects the luxuriance of the foliage. Just as a log which has been set afire froths and pants at its as yet untouched end, and like water purified of witchcraft by exorcism, so, compelled to give abode to God Almighty, the heathen stone emitted on the outside a grimacing and demoniac vermin, and the vomiting gargoyles and the tall grass of fruitless flowers. As the hour of Scandal draws closer, the swarming of unbelievers becomes more vivacious and more intense and it is as if the entire sap of the Church were to be spent on this parasitic mistletoe. Lo, it is not long before it accepts strange adornments. The Gothic soul dies out.

But not before having given to France the entire framework of her worship, like the completion of the system of cities and towns, born, one by one, out of the whirlpool, at the confluence of rivers and roads. No latent prayer included in the now voiceless site, no religious fief, which did not pledge allegiance to a certain tall tower. Today, the church is but an anonymous oratory, a common piece of furniture, like a confessional or a prie-Dieu of the material of devotion. But, at first, the legends of visions of oak-trees or in thorns, of statues found on fallow lands, of baptismal springs, suddenly gushing out of the earth, give a fair idea of the necessity which, in old days, joined the rough soil to the foundations clinging to it. The length of time required for the construction of the edifice, its nourishment drawn from the very soil on which it grew, enabled it to take on the peculiar flavor of its natal land, so to say; it was the expression of the special mode of local permanence under the sun, the eruption of the autochthonous testimony. Over and above the roofs and the walls of the City, the Cathedral towered high over the diocese. The traveller could see it from afar, like the sacred coat of

arms of the area, depicted over the countryside or delineated against the sky.

When the apostles of the Gauls died, the very pulpits
from which they had preached, the Cathedrals, continued their teachings and are still bestowing them upon
all, above all human voices. Just as people go to the
sacred shrines to seek recovery from their ills, so it seems
that only the eternal shadows treasured by these old
walls can melt the envelope of our personal night, dissolve our noisy deafness in the silence of the Good
Tidings. It cannot be said that the Cathedral is made
for prayers; rather, it is prayer's pompous ceremonial.
Stepping over its threshold is, like opening the breviary,
to become incorporated into a deprecative arrangement,
into the official supplication prepared for all human-
ity. Just as the liturgy, in days of old, used to vary
according to the diocese, so does one metropolis vary
from the other. At Notre Dame, more than anywhere
else, in the very midst of the filth of Paris, like
Jeremiah, in his cistern engulfed under deep waters, you
will have a taste of Death; how reassuring, if you raise
your head, to see, instead of the sun, these enduring
large streaked roses, which seem to absorb, to suspend,
trophy-like—the better to exclude it—the light which
might otherwise gain access. Rheims, streaming with
balsams, is ready for other consecrations still, for receiving more than the ancient Kings. But among all others,
Chartres is truly Our Lady's Church. How magnani-

mously ample her choir opens before our eyes! She is
blessed with the virtue of the Most High; she is the
exaltation of humility, she is penitence in full glory!
She is suave and unique. Honorable vessel, receptacle
of orthodoxy, spiritual secret, vase of prudence, famous
sanctuary of devotion! Full of grace, she can be seen
from all points, completing the poor old city entirely,
within herself; she draws from it, as if through roots, she
adapts to it, as if joined by tenon and mortise, she rises
and partakes of the movement of all roofs, and, her two
equal spires confirming the spreading of the city, she
does not fail the injured eye, which seeks passage to the
skies. The perpetual winds have made it impossible for
the sculptors to succeed on her highest walls: just as
the gramineous plants and moss try out the old walls,
and both houseleek and gilliflower take advantage of all
good nooks, here ornaments and statues are limited to
the places where pent-roofs and cornices provide a
semblance of shelter. The Saints have taken refuge
under the porches to such an extent that it became necessary to reserve for them, on the northern side, this
ample hallway, where, on Sundays, after mass, the
townsfolk come, informally, to get used to their com-
pany. As for the steeples, the one which is sheltered from
the wind erects a rigid and naked cone; the other, like a
stake planted against the tide, stops all the wrecks adrift
through the boundless air, the long mists and the tena-
cious smoke, and the angels, and the crows; they become

entangled, they wind around its base. The venerable forest, whose peaks seem tied to each other, as by the entanglement of their fruits, have permitted these two stalks to go free. The seed, here too, is the grain of mystic black mustard! go in and you shall be able to adore the little statue found, in times of old, beneath the ground, like a black kernel.

Today, a new shoot, does not bring other shades. Once upon a time, the unanimous crowd convening for the sacrifice, asked from the church, vast as a purgatory, nothing but the dimness and the security of its protective abyss. Faith becomes cloudy as daylight penetrates from the outside. Now, the remaining faithful see, before their eyes, in full daylight, the altar in all its details—gold and linen—of its liturgical adornments, and the closed tabernacle, and the cross, severely obvious. For, when the Protestant blasphemy assured people that each man was master of his justification and denied the power of the priest to sanctify by the touch of his hand, the believers wanted to see the host more clearly, and day entered the sanctuary. If the presence of Christ in the consecrated elements were not solely— as the innovators would have it—a sort of alimentary luxury, a mystery confined to the contact of the palate with the tongue, it became important that the worship should not be limited to the liturgical act, but that permanent residence and honor be extended to the Eucharist among us. Forthwith, on the steady stone, Rome erected the enormous dome. Already during the seventeenth and eighteenth centuries, churches became huge audience and reception halls, forever open refuges, confidential parlors, furnished according to the taste guiding us in our own homes. In our days, the Sacré-Coeur represents the final and complete achievement of the new idea: an always visible God, an always present people; the exaltation of the bread, the display of the secret heart. But no more can be said here.

INDEX